NITA DEPOSITION PRACTICUM EXERCISE

The NITA Practicum Series is designed to be an effective tool to help attorneys and students develop and improve effective **Advocacy Skills**.

The Practicum exercises are self-contained and have all necessary information. No outside research is required.

NITA Advocacy Training Options

In addition to depositions, this Practicum exercise may be used in the following Advocacy Training Programs:

• Arbitration • Trial (Court/Jury) • Negotiation • Mediation • Motions/Oral Argument • Expert Witnesses

This Practicum exercise contains the following:

- *Party and Witness Statements/Depositions*
- *Procedural and Factual History*
- *The Facts*
- *Applicable Law*
- *The Pleadings*
- *Case and Strategic Analysis*

    The case and strategic analysis is a preliminary guide, supplying the basis for a more sophisticated analysis, preparation, and performance.

Learning Materials

The Learning Materials are located at the end of this exercise.

- *Planning Guide and Checklist*

    The Planning Guide and Checklist is an outline that assists in the preparation of legal substance and presentation. It provides the basis for more detailed planning.

- *Learning Objectives*

    The Learning Objectives provide a method to measure achievement.

    Oral—assist in planning and delivering the assigned oral skill.

    Written—assist in developing and presenting both written and oral skills.

A Practicum Exercise

for

NITA

TORT

PERSONAL INJURY

Plaintiff's Materials

Advocacy Training Options

- Trial (Court / Jury)
- Negotiation
- Mediation
- Motions / Oral Argument
- Expert Witnesses

Helen Darngood (Plaintiff)

v.

Mel Landers and
Picket Up Delivery Services (PUDS) (Defendants)

HELEN DARNGOOD (PLAINTIFF)
V.
MEL LANDERS AND
PICKET UP DELIVERY SERVICES (PUDS) (DEFENDANTS)

Plaintiff's Materials

by

John O. Sonsteng and Linda M. Thorstad

with Jennifer W. Miller

NATIONAL INSTITUTE FOR TRIAL ADVOCACY

Reprint Permission
National Institute for Trial Advocacy
1685 38th Street, Suite 200
Boulder, CO 80301
Phone: (800) 225-6482
Fax: (720) 890-7069
E-mail: permissions@nita.org

FBA1182
ISBN 978-1-60156-182-4

Printed in the United States of America

CONTENTS

Exhibit List [Exhibits located on CD]

  Exhibit 1:   Collective Bargaining Agreement between
              Picket Up Delivery Services and IATW
                (Witnesses: Mel Landers, Perry Reinhart, Homer Picket)

  Exhibit 2:   Picket Up Delivery Services Special Rule—Traffic Violation Policy: B(1)
                (Witnesses: Mel Landers, Perry Reinhart, Homer Picket)

  Exhibit 3:   Memo from Homer Picket to Employee (Landers) File
                (Witnesses: Homer Picket and Mel Landers)

  Exhibit 4:   Letter of Reprimand from Juliette Nelson-Picket to Mel Landers
                (Witnesses: Mel Landers, Perry Reinhart)

  Exhibit 5:   PUDS Van Specifications
                (By Stipulation—All Parties)

  Exhibit 6:   Picture of Mussel Pot
                (Witness: Cooper Earle)

  Exhibit 7:   Photograph of Stop and Walk Signals
                (Witnesses: Helen Darngood, Cooper Earle, Mel Landers)

  Exhibit 8:   Speed Calculation
                (By Stipulation—All Parties)

  Exhibit 9:   Photographs of PUDS Uniform Shirt (Front and Back)
                (Witnesses: Cooper Earle, Mel Landers, Perry Reinhart)

Exhibit 10:   Photograph of Downtown Nita City—Looking North on Seventh Street from Grand Avenue
      (Witnesses: Helen Darngood, Cooper Earle, Mel Landers)

Exhibit 11:   Accident Diagram With Picket Up Delivery Services Van
      (Witnesses: Mel Landers, Helen Darngood, Cooper Earle)

Exhibit 12:   Accident Diagram Without Picket Up Delivery Services Van
      (Witnesses: Mel Landers, Helen Darngood, Cooper Earle)

Exhibit 13:   Alcohol Influence Report
      (By Stipulation—All Parties)

Exhibit 14:   Intoxilyzer Test Record
      (By Stipulation—All Parties)

Exhibit 15:   Alcohol Impairment Charts
      (By Stipulation—All Parties)

Exhibit 16:   Helen Darngood's Resignation Letter
      (Witness: Helen Darngood)

Exhibit 17:   Expert Medical Report, C.R. Strickland, MD
      (By Stipulation—All Parties)

Exhibit 18:   Manual for The Wheeled Vehicle Driver—Departments of Army and Air Force (Appendix C)
      (By Stipulation—All Parties)

ACKNOWLEDGMENTS

This NITA Practicum Exercise was successfully designed and tested at William Mitchell College of Law, St. Paul, Minnesota.

We gratefully acknowledge William Mitchell College of Law Legal Practicum and Advanced Advocacy students and adjunct faculty who critiqued this exercise and suggested improvements.

The following students from William Mitchell College of Law made major contributions to the NITA Practicum exercises: Sarah Bennett, Christine Eid, Lauralee Fritz, Mary Harens, Anne Howarth, Briana Isiminger, Jan Jeske, Kelly Martinez, Jessica Nault, Taylor Tarvestad, Jacob Thompson, Maureen Ventura, and Chong Ye.

Special thanks to our families who stood beside us through the NITA Practicum Exercise development, creation, editing, re-editing, proofing and re-proofing for days, weeks, months and in some instances years. We are grateful for their involvement, suggestions, patience, inspiration, and encouragement.

Diane, Michael, Stacy, David, and Molly

John and Troy Thorstad

Jonny, Jake, and Jada Miller

VERY IMPORTANT

DIRECTIONS FOR DETERMINING DATES, AGES, AND APPLICABLE LAW

In order to keep this exercise current and workable for any time and place, *dates, ages, and statutes **must** be inserted where indicated by a blank line and a bold instruction in parentheses.*

Dates

Use a current calendar. Dates are to be calculated from the date assigned by the instructor. Should an event occur on a holiday, the holiday should be ignored unless specifically indicated by the exercise or the instructor.

Dates are NOT an issue in an exercise unless specifically indicated by the instructor.

The following formula will permit correct dates to be inserted where necessary.

- All dates following the assignment of the exercise are indicated by a "plus" (+) sign, followed by the number of days, weeks, months, or years to be counted:

  (day +1), (week +1), (month +1), (year +1)

- All dates preceding the assignment of the exercise are indicated by a "minus" (-) sign, followed by the number of days, weeks, months, or years to be counted:

  (day -1), (week -1), (month -1), (year -1)

- The date assigned by instructor is:

  (day 0), (week 0), (month 0), and (year 0).

- NEVER count the current day, week, or month when calculating the dates.

How to Calculate and Insert the Dates

Example 1:

- The exercise is assigned on **Friday, July 29, 2011**.

  ‣ *Before* the date is inserted, the exercise reads as follows:

*We purchased the stock on _____ (**Wednesday, Week -3**).*

- Do not count the current week. Count back three weeks. The date that must be inserted is July 6, 2011.

  ‣ *After* inserting this date, the exercise will now read:

*We purchased the stock on July 6, 2011 (**Wednesday, Week -3**).*

Example 2:

- The exercise is assigned on **Monday, August 8, 2011.**

  ‣ *Before* the date is inserted, the exercise reads as follows:

I bought the house on _____ (**1st Wednesday, Month -28**).

- Do not count the current month. Count back 28 months. The date that must be inserted is Wednesday, April 2, 2009.

  ‣ After inserting this date, the exercise will now read:

I bought the house on <u>Wednesday, April 2, 2009</u> (**1st Wednesday, Month -28**).

Ages

The ages of clients and other people may be found throughout the exercise.

Example:

- I was born on April 18, _____(**Year -48**).

This indicates that the person would be forty-eight years old.

Applicable Law

Unless otherwise indicated by the exercise, the law of your jurisdiction will apply.

Example:

- *Before* the current statutory reference is inserted, the exercise reads as follows:

  The above-named juvenile is alleged to be delinquent pursuant to _____ (**state statute**) because the juvenile has violated a state/local law as follows . . . .

- *After* inserting the current statutory reference, the exercise will now read:

  The above-named juvenile is alleged to be delinquent pursuant to <u>Nita Stat. 609.015</u> (**state statute**) because the juvenile has violated a state/local law as follows . . . .

Darngood v. Landers and PUDS, Plaintiff

PROCEDURAL AND FACTUAL HISTORY

Assume the days and dates in the exercise are accurate.

The following facts and procedures are agreed to by the parties and must be accepted by them. These facts may be considered as agreed upon evidence and may be used in the opening statement and closing argument.

Introduction

This lawsuit arises out of a traffic accident that occurred on December 23, _____(**Year -2**), in the pedestrian crosswalk at the intersection of Seventh Street and Smith Avenue in Nita City, Nita. The plaintiff, Helen Darngood, was struck by a Picket Up Delivery Services van driven by the defendant, Mel Landers. A negligence action has been brought by Helen Darngood against Mel Landers and Picket Up Delivery Services. Darngood's husband, children, and former company are *not* parties to this lawsuit.

All parties agree that Mel Landers was acting in the scope of Landers's duties while working for Picket Up Delivery Services at the time of the accident. Darngood alleges that Landers was negligent as the driver of the Picket Up Delivery Services van and that Landers did not drive as an ordinary, careful, and prudent person would drive under the circumstances. Darngood alleges that Landers drove the Picket Up Delivery Services van negligently into a crosswalk, striking Darngood and causing her severe injuries.

Landers and Picket Up Delivery Services deny negligence. They claim that the vehicle driven by Landers entered the intersection on a yellow light, that the vehicle proceeded through the intersection as permitted by law, and that Darngood was 100 percent contributorily negligent in that she crossed negligently in front of the van. Thus, Landers as the driver of the delivery vehicle is not liable for negligence nor is Picket Up Delivery Services liable under the doctrine of respondeat superior.

Darngood, at the time of the accident, was the President and CEO of Darngood Electronics, earning an annual salary of $200,000. At the time of this lawsuit Darngood cannot work and has resigned from the company. Darngood does not remember the accident or the time immediately following while she was in rehabilitation (see Dr. Strickland's statement). Darngood acknowledges that she cannot perform up to her usual standards and states in her deposition, "It is best for me to resign from the company."

Background

Darngood Electronics

Darngood Electronics is the third largest electronic retail chain in the United States, with annual sales exceeding $300 million. Joseph "Joe" Darngood began selling appliances in _____(**Year -25**) in Nita City, Nita. From there, the company branched out and now has sixty-five retail stores across the United States and Canada that merchandise a wide variety of electronics, household appliances, and music. Always a leader and innovator, Darngood's name has become synonymous with quality merchandise, dedicated employees, superb customer service, and community involvement at each franchise location. Since the company's inception, it has been a tradition each holiday season for the Darngood stores to add to the festivities of the communities in which its stores are located by presenting lavishly decorated store windows and animated displays.

Helen Darngood became the President and CEO of Darngood Electronics when her father, Joe, died five years ago. Helen is married to George Carpenter, and together they have three children—daughters Krista and Kari, aged twelve and eleven, respectively, and son James, age eight. Since Helen's accident and subsequent absence from the company, Margaret Hanson has been named the Acting President and CEO for Darngood Electronics.

Before the accident, Darngood Electronics was negotiating an agreement with St. Helens Worldwide Technology. The chief negotiators were Helen Darngood for Darngood Electronics and Fran DeGrew, President and CEO of St. Helens Worldwide Technology. Under the contract, which would become effective on January 1, _____(**Year +2**), Darngood would begin selling one million of the St. Helens' computer security systems for commercial, industrial, and personal computer markets. That contract would be in effect if the sales of the computer security system reached an annual sale of $100,000 worth of products for _____ (**Year +1**) through the marketing efforts of Darngood Electronics. It is expected to do so. The potential profit for Darngood on this product alone is projected to be well in excess of $10 million annually.

The contract requires St. Helens to perform all annual updates to the security system and sets out the specifics of the updates. The update specifics were proposed by St. Helens as a part of the contract. The contract states that the retail sale value of the security system will be $149.95, and Darngood will purchase it at a cost of $49.95. The price may increase depending on the results of market surveys conducted by St. Helens and Darngood and will be pegged to those results. Updates to the security system will be available to previous purchasers of the security system at a price of $30.00. That agreement is now on hold pending the return of Helen Darngood to the management team or a successful restructuring of Darngood management.

In addition, at the time of the accident, negotiations were underway between Darngood Electronics, St. Helens Worldwide Technology and Picket Up Delivery Services. The negotiations regarded the award of an exclusive contract to Picket Up Delivery Services for the nationwide shipping and delivery of St. Helens's security system products to all Darngood Electronics retail outlets. These negotiations have also been put on hold.

Picket Up Delivery Services (PUDS)

Picket Up Delivery Services, located in Nita City, Nita, is solely owned by Homer Picket. Homer Picket is assisted by the vice president, who is his daughter, Juliette Nelson-Picket, age forty-one. Picket Up Delivery Services is the fourth largest delivery company in the United States and is growing rapidly. The company has an annual gross revenue of more than $80 million. Homer Picket started the company after serving thirty years in the Marine Corps. PUDS started small, with five employees twenty-three years ago; it currently has 400 employees and a growing clientele. Its odd name and slogan have caught the fancy of the American public.

Description of the Scene

Seventh Street is a busy arterial street that runs north and south through the downtown commercial and shopping district of Nita City. Many of the east/west cross streets that intersect Seventh Street are also busy. (See police accident map/diagram.)

There are traffic semaphores on each corner of the five blocks in either direction of the accident site (Seventh Street and Smith Avenue). The east/west semaphore lights on the corner cannot be seen from persons looking north or south. The north/south semaphore lights on the corner cannot be seen from persons looking east or west. The semaphore lights are all timed and do not change at the same time. Large metropolitan buses, which are white with red lettering, run on Seventh Street. All streets have automobile traffic and regular street lighting.

At 7:00 p.m. on the December 23, ____(**Year -2**), it was dark and the street lights were on. Crowds of pedestrian shoppers were walking up and down the streets wearing their typical winter outfits—hats, scarves, jackets, and heavy sweaters. All the shop and store windows along Seventh Street had large plate glass windows, behind which were holiday displays containing multicolored packages, Christmas trees, lights, Santa Clauses, elves, and other holiday decorations and ornaments. Evergreen garlands hung above the streets every fifty feet. On the sidewalks were three-foot high, red plastic candles on the corner of each street and one in the middle of the block. The candles had faux yellow and white illuminated flames and yellow wax dripping down the sides. King's Department Store (on the southwest corner of Seventh and Smith) outlined its building in red lights. Darngood Electronics outlined its building in gold.

Cooper Earle, who owns a bookstore near the accident, is a witness to the accident. Earle had a glass of wine prior to the accident. Earle was carrying a heavy mussel pot that was a gift for Earle's spouse when walking towards the intersection where the accident occurred.

Police Accident Report

The police officer who investigated the scene of the accident, R.J. Moore, is **not available** to testify. The police report is hearsay and is not admissible in a trial under any circumstances. The police report may be used in a deposition as appropriate. Both parties agree that the police report is accurate.

Diagrams

The diagrams in the police report *are accurate and admissible*. Both parties, without further foundation, may use the diagram at trial. However, the size of the PUDS van is not to scale. This inaccuracy may be solved through jury instructions, by removing the van entirely from the diagram, or by replacing the van with a more accurate depiction.

Supplementary Report and Alcohol Influence Report

The Supplementary Report and Alcohol Influence Report *are admissible*. The reports can be used by both parties as exhibits at trial and during any deposition. The Supplementary Report and the Alcohol Influence Report should have an exhibit number and be referred to by that number.

Toxicologist Report

The toxicologist, Sing Chen, is **not available** as a witness at trial. The toxicologist report *is admissible* (see below). Either party can use the report as an exhibit at trial and during any deposition. The report should have an exhibit number and be referred to by that number. The results of the report are accurate. Slight variations in readings are to be expected and are well within the range of acceptability. In this exercise the .059 BAC reading for Mel Landers cannot be challenged.

Medical Report

When expert witness examinations *are not* a part of this exercise, the report of the expert witness (Dr. C.R. Strickland) *is* admissible. It is agreed to be accurate by all parties, and the foundation for introduction of the expert's report is by stipulation of all parties. The doctor's report should be marked as an exhibit and entered into evidence before opening statements. Both parties may refer to the report in opening statement and final argument. In a trial the judge *may* provide the report to the jury.

Traffic and Walk Signals

The traffic signals cannot be seen from the side, only by directly facing them—e.g., the north/south traffic and pedestrians cannot see the east/west signals and vice versa. The traffic signal changes from green to yellow to red. The yellow light remains on for 3.5 seconds. The light then turns to red for two seconds for traffic in all directions, after which the light for one direction remains red and for the opposite direction becomes green. When the light turns green, the pedestrian signal changes from an orange (stop) hand to a white (walk) figure.

PUDS Delivery Van Specifications

The Picket Up Delivery Services van driven by Mel Landers weighs less than 26,000 pounds and is therefore not a commercial vehicle. Standard alcohol driving restrictions apply.

The PUDS vans are especially built for the company. The vans have weight and dimension sizes as follows:

Weight:

curb weight (lbs): 5340.

External Dimensions:

overall length (mm/in): 5893/232.0

overall width (mm/in): 2014/79.3

overall height (mm/in): 2149/84.6

wheelbase (mm/in): 3505/138.0

curb to curb turning circle (mm/ft): 14630/48.0.

Speed Calculation

- A vehicle traveling 60 miles per hour travels a distance of 88 feet per second.
- A vehicle traveling 15 miles per hour travels a distance of 22 feet per second.
- The intersection in this exercise is 66 feet wide.
- It is 5.5 seconds from the time the light turned yellow for Mel Landers until it turned green for Helen Darngood.
- A vehicle traveling 66 feet in 5.5 seconds will travel 12.363 feet in one second and the vehicle will be moving at the rate of 8.18 miles per hour.

Issues Raised

(These issues do not limit participants. Other appropriate issues may be raised.)

A. Negligence

B. Contributory Negligence

C. Damages

- Plaintiff (Helen Darngood)
  - Physical
  - Mental
  - Economic

Darngood v. Landers and PUDS, Plaintiff

D. Liability

- Defendant (Mel Landers)

  – Negligence

- Defendant (Picket Up Delivery Services)

  – Homer Picket

  – Respondeat Superior

E. Not Parties to this Lawsuit

- Family of Plaintiff

  – George Carpenter

  – Krista Carpenter, Kari Carpenter, James Carpenter

- Darngood Electronics

F. Traffic Laws (See Appendix for Statutes)

Witnesses

(*Cooper Earle, Mel Landers, and Perry Reinhart may be male or female.*)

Unless otherwise advised, parties may not call any of the other parties' witnesses in their case-in-chief.

Plaintiff

Helen Darngood

Cooper Earle

Margaret Hanson (damages only)

George Carpenter (damages only)

Dr. C.R. Strickland (damages only) (see Expert Witnesses below)

Defendant

Mel Landers

Perry Reinhart

Homer Picket

Juliette Nelson-Picket (not available for trial)

Expert Witnesses

Experts are only called as witnesses when expert witness examination is part of the exercise. Expert witness examinations add thirty minutes per side (twenty minutes for direct examination and ten minutes for cross-examination).

When expert witness examinations *are* a part of the exercise, the admissibility and use of expert witness reports are governed by the agreed upon rules of evidence.

When expert witness examinations *are not* a part of this exercise, the report of the expert witness (Dr. C.R. Strickland) *is* admissible. All parties agree that it is accurate, and the foundation for introduction of the expert's report is by stipulation of all parties. The doctor's report should be marked as an exhibit and entered into evidence before opening statements. Both parties may refer to the report in opening statement and final argument. In a trial, the judge *may* provide the report to the jury.

Plaintiff

Helen (nickname "Pretty") Darngood

Role:	Injured in accident/plaintiff.
Age:	37 years old, born April 18, _____**(Year -37)**.
Married:	Married, George Carpenter, age 43.
	Three children: daughters: Krista, age 12; Kari, age 11; son: James, age 8.
Education:	BA, English and Communications, Stanford University, _____**(Year - 15)**.
	MBA, Nita State University,_____**(Year -12)**.

Employment:

- Operations Assistant, Darngood Electronics, _____**(Year -12)** to _____**(Year -10)**.
- Operations Manager, Darngood Electronics, _____**(Year -10)** to _____**(Year -8)**.
- Vice-President Operations and Business Manager, Darngood Electronics, ____**(Year -8)** to _____**(Year -5)**.
- President and CEO, Darngood Electronics, _____**(Year -5)** to **June 10,** _____**(Year -1)**.

George Carpenter

Role:	Helen Darngood's husband.
Age:	43 years old, born February 28, _____**(Year -43)**.
Married:	Married, Helen Darngood.
	Three children: daughters: Krista, age 12; Kari, age 11; son: James, age 8.
Education:	MD, Louisiana State University School of Medicine,_____**(Year -10)**.
Employment:	

- Psychiatrist and tenured professor in Department of Psychiatry at Nita State University.

Margaret Hanson

Role:	Assumed Helen Darngood's position at Darngood Electronics.
Age:	52 years old, born May 12, _____**(Year -52)**.
Married:	Divorced. One son, Sam, age 32. Two grandsons, ages 6 and 5.
Education:	BA, Economics, Nita State University.

Darngood v. Landers and PUDS, Plaintiff

Employment:

- Vice President, Darngood Electronics, _____(Year -10) to _____(Year -1).

- Acting President and CEO, Darngood Electronics, June 15, _____(Year -1) to present.

Cooper Earle

Role:	Accident Witness.
Age:	37 years old, born November 10, _____(Year -37).
Married:	Married. Two daughters, ages 10, 8.
Education:	BA, major in Classic Literature, minor in Art and Music, Harvard University, _____(Year -15).
	MBA, Business Management, Nita State University, _____(Year -12).

Employment:

- Owner/Manager, Cooper, Grumble, and Green, Booksellers, _____(Year -11) to present.

Defendants

Mel Landers

Role:	Driver of PUDS van involved in accident/defendant.
Age:	35 years old, born July 15, _____(Year -35).
Married:	Widowed. One son, William, age 12.
Education:	Nita High School, _____(Year -17).
	Junior, Nita State University, currently enrolled in evening classes working towards BA in Business.

Employment:

- U.S. Army, Transport Division, _____(Year -17) to _____(Year -13).
- Jake's Moving Company, _____(Year -13) to _____(Year -10).
- Picket Up Delivery Services, _____(Year -10) to _____(Year -0).

Picket Up Delivery Services (PUDS)

Age:	Company formed twenty-three years ago/defendant.
Location:	1965 Industrial Blvd., Nita City, Nita
Owner:	Homer Picket, 73 years old.
Vice President:	Juliette Nelson-Picket, age 41.
Annual Gross Revenue:	More than $80 million.
Size:	Fourth largest delivery company in the United States.

Homer Picket

Role: Owner of PUDS.

Age: 73 years old, born December 23, _____ **(Year -73)**.

Married: Widowed. One daughter, Juliette, age 41.

Education: Nita High School, _____ **(Year -55)**.

Employment:

- U.S. Marine Corp. (ret. Master Gunnery Sgt), _____ **(Year -53) to** _____ **(Year -23)**.
- Owner, Picket Up Delivery Services, _____ **(Year -23) to present**.

Perry Reinhart

Role: Coworker of Mel Landers.

Age: 26 years old, born August 23, _____ **(Year -26)**.

Married: Married. Two sons.

Education: Nita High School, _____ **(Year -8)**.

Employment:

- Jake's Moving Company, _____ **(Year -8) to** _____ **(Year -6)**.
- Picket Up Delivery Services, _____ **(Year -6) to present**.

Juliette Nelson-Picket

Role: Vice-President of PUDS.

Age: 41 years old, born April 21, _____ **(Year -41)**.

Married: Unmarried.

Education: MBA, Business Management, Ohio State University, _____ **(Year -15)**.

Employment:

- Vice-President, Picket Up Delivery Services, _____ **(Year -14) to present**.

Police Officer

R.J. Moore is deceased.

Expert Medical Witness

Dr. C.R. Strickland

Age: 49.

Married: Married. Four children.

Education: MD, Johns Hopkins University,_____(Year -20).

Internship, Baltimore General Hospital,_____**(Year -20) to** _____**(Year -18)**.

Residency, Nita State University Hospital,_____**(Year -18) to** _____**(Year -14)**.

Employment:

- Private Practice in Neurosurgery, _____**(Year -13) to present**.

- Teaching Physician and Neurosurgeon, Nita State University Hospital, _____**(Year -10) to present**.

Expert Toxicologist Witness

Sing Chen (not available for trial)

Age: 58.

Married: Divorced.

Education: MS, Chemistry, McGill University, Montreal, Canada, _____**(Year -33)**.

Employment:

- State Bureau of Criminal Apprehension, Toxicologist, _____**(Year -32) to present**.

Toxicologist Report accompanies the Police Accident Report. Toxicologist Report is agreed to by all parties.

Party and Witness Depositions and/or Statement

The depositions and/or statements are comprised of information provided by witnesses and have been adopted by them as true and correct. Accordingly, they may be used as is appropriate under the rules of evidence. When testifying, each witness may add only nonsubstantial facts that are consistent with the case file. Significant substantive facts may not be added.

Exhibits and Documents

The exhibits and documents are all authentic. Witness testimony provides both legal and persuasive foundation for exhibits. The exhibits may be marked separately (i.e., Exhibit 1, Exhibit 2, etc.) or the page number in the upper right-hand corner of each page can serve as the exhibit number. If the exhibit has more than one page, the first page of the exhibit can serve as the exhibit number and the number of pages contained in the exhibit can be found at the top of the page.

All exhibits should be offered for admission and be received into evidence before the exhibit can be used. The agreed-upon rules of evidence apply in regard to admission of exhibits.

THE
FACTS

DETAILED TIMELINE OF SIGNIFICANT DATES

(Year -3)

- **Jan. 1**   PUDS' Traffic Violation Policy (Article 28) goes into effect.
- **June 15**   Landers receives speeding ticket.
- **Nov. 15**   Landers receives traffic violation.

(Year -2)

- **Dec. 23**   PUDS' Holiday Party—3:00–7:00 p.m.
- **Dec. 23**   Helen Darngood struck by PUDS' delivery van driven by Mel Landers at approximately 7:00 p.m.
- **Dec. 24**   Police Report filed by Officer R.J. Moore.

(Year -1)

- **June 10**   Helen Darngood resigns as President and CEO of Darngood Electronics.

(Year -0)

- **1st Monday, Month -5**   Summons and Complaint.
- **3rd Monday, Month -5**   Answer.
- **Month -2**   Depositions completed.
- **Week -6**   Joint Statement of Case.

Picket Up Delivery Services

The Big Green Transport Machine

TO: PUDS Employees

FROM: Juliette Nelson-Picket, Vice President

DATE: **January 15, _____(Year -5)**

RE: Collective Bargaining Agreement between Picket Up Delivery Services and IATW

Picket Up Delivery Services and the International Association of Transport Workers (IATW) have approved a Collective Bargaining Agreement by a vote of the membership of the IATW and the Board of Directors of Picket Up Delivery Services. The Collective Bargaining Agreement is in effect as of this date. It is attached.

COLLECTIVE BARGAINING AGREEMENT
(Page 1 of 2)

Article 28—Collective Bargaining Agreement between Picket Up Delivery Services and International Association of Transport Workers (IATW) Local #512

Adopted January 15, _____ (Year -5)

[The Agreement has been edited for this Exercise.]

A. Nothing in this Agreement is intended to circumscribe or modify the existing right of Picket Up Delivery Services to:

  (1) direct the work of its employees.

  (2) hire, promote, assign, transfer, and retain as to position with the Company.

  (3) demote, suspend, reduce in pay, or discharge employees for just cause.

  (4) maintain the efficiency of company operations.

  (5) take actions as may be necessary to carry out the mission and vision of the Company.

  (6) determine the methods, means, and personnel by which operations are to be carried on.

  (7) develop and implement reasonable* rules of employment including schedules and time keeping.

  (8) promulgate reasonable* reporting and record keeping obligations and procedures in policies adopted under the Collective Bargaining Agreement.

*Reasonable: being in accordance with reason; not extreme or excessive; moderate and fair, and possessing sound judgment.

B. Disciplinary actions may, at the employer's discretion, include warnings, suspensions, and discharges. Any employee disciplined or discharged shall be entitled to file a grievance through the Employee's Union. The grievance must set out the basis for the grievance. If requested in writing by the Union, an expedited hearing will be held with the Union within thirty (30) days of the Disciplinary Action or Discharge Violation.

  1. **Violation of critical work rules.** Critical work rules are defined as rules that endanger health or safety. A violation of a critical work rule may subject the Employee to immediate termination.

  2. **Violation of noncritical work rules.** Noncritical work rules are defined as rules that do not endanger health or safety.

  Steps to Discipline:

  Step 1: A first violation. When an Employee violates a noncritical work rule, the Employee shall receive an oral notice. Verification of this oral notice shall be placed in writing in the Employee's personnel file.

  Step 2: A second violation. Employee shall receive a written reprimand to be placed in the Employee's file. The Employee shall meet with the Human Resources Director.

  Step 3: A third violation subjects the Employee to a written reprimand and a suspension without pay for up to 30 days. The Employee and the Union Steward may meet with the Human Resources Director prior to the enforcement of the suspension.

  Step 4: A fourth violation of a noncritical work rule will subject the Employee to the immediate termination of employment. The basis for the discipline, including termination, must be set out in writing and must state all grounds for the discipline. The written notice of discipline must be provided to the Employee and the International Association of Transport Workers (IATW) representing the Employee.

C. The Parties to the Collective Bargaining Agreement may agree that this matter may be resolved through negotiation or mediation. Absent such an agreement, the matter will be resolved through arbitration. However, when an Employee is terminated the Employee may elect to have the matter heard by a judge or jury. (See E. below.)

COLLECTIVE BARGAINING AGREEMENT
(Page 2 of 2)

D. Arbitration

- Burden of Proof: The Employer shall have the burden of proof by a preponderance of the evidence that there was just cause for discipline of the Employee and just cause for the degree of discipline.

- Disciplinary arbitrators shall render determinations of a violation of work rules and the appropriateness of proposed penalties, and shall have the authority to resolve a claimed failure to follow the procedural provisions of this Agreement. Disciplinary arbitrators shall neither add to, subtract from, nor modify the provisions of this Agreement. In an arbitration, the Employee may be terminated, suspended, or reinstated with or without back pay. Additional damages are not available in an arbitration.

- The Employee (grievant) shall be represented by the Union.

- The Employer shall present the first opening statement and the concluding final argument.

- The Employee (grievant) shall not have a rebuttal final argument.

- The arbitrator shall determine the Rules of Evidence that shall apply.

E. Trial to Judge or Jury

- If an Employee is terminated, the Employee may elect to have the matter heard by a judge or jury.

- The Employee must notify the Employer in writing of this election within ten (10) days of the Employee's termination. If the tenth day falls on a Saturday, Sunday or legal, national or state holiday, the tenth day shall be the next full work day.

- Upon election to try the matter to a judge or jury, the Employee must file a complaint in state court within thirty (30) days of this election.

- The Employer must file an answer within thirty (30) days of receiving notice of the complaint.

- The Union shall not be required to represent the Employee in a trial. (The Union may choose to represent the Employee.)

- Burden of Proof: The Employee shall have the burden of proof by a preponderance of the evidence that there was insufficient cause for termination.

- In a trial to a judge or jury, the Employee may seek damages in addition to the remedies provided by the Collective Bargaining Agreement.

- The Employee shall be the plaintiff, and the Employer shall be the defendant.

- The Employee shall present the first opening statement and the concluding final argument.

- The Employer shall not have a rebuttal final argument.

- The Employee must present evidence first.

- The Rules of Evidence, Procedure, and Law of the jurisdiction where the complaint is filed shall govern but shall not amend any terms of this agreement.

F. Discovery Depositions

- The Employer and the employee may take discovery depositions of witnesses or parties.

- The depositions are limited to three per side.

- A deposition of a witness or a party may not exceed thirty (30) minutes.

- Upon written application and with good cause shown, the thirty (30) minute time limit for taking a deposition and the number of persons to be deposed may be increased.

Darngood v. Landers and PUDS, Plaintiff

Picket Up Delivery Services

The Big Green Transport Machine

TO: PUDS Employees

FROM: Juliette Nelson-Picket, Vice President

DATE: **January 1, _____(Year -3)**

RE: Article 28 of the Collective Bargaining Agreement

Under Article 28 of the Collective Bargaining Agreement adopted **January 15, ____(Year -5)**, we have instituted Special Rule—Traffic Violation Policy B(1) defining a Critical Work Rule Policy for Drivers of PUDS' vehicles. The special rule is effective immediately.

Attached Special Rule—Traffic Violation Policy B(1)

TRAFFIC VIOLATION POLICY

FOR PICKET UP DELIVERY SERVICES

TRUCK DRIVERS

Special Rule: B(1)

Implemented under Article 28 of the Collective Bargaining Agreement on

January 1, _____ (Year -3)

CRITICAL WORK RULE POLICY FOR DRIVERS OF PUDS' VEHICLES

Employee traffic violations shall be reported to company management and are subject to discipline. The policy implemented shall be as follows:

- The first traffic violation that an employee receives, whether the violation occurs while the employee operates a personal vehicle off duty or while operating a Picket Up Delivery Services vehicle on duty, will justify a two-day suspension without pay and a written letter of reprimand.

- A second traffic violation by an employee within five years of the first traffic violation, whether the violation occurs while the employee operates a personal vehicle off duty or while operating a Picket Up Delivery Services vehicle on duty, may result in a letter of reprimand and suspension of up to thirty days without pay. A violation resulting in personal injury or death justifies further discipline including termination of employment.

- A third traffic violation by an employee within five years of the first traffic violation, whether the violation occurs while the employee operates a personal vehicle off duty or while operating a Picket Up Delivery Services vehicle on duty, may result in the termination of the employee.

Picket Up Delivery Services

The Big Green Transport Machine

INTEROFFICE MEMO

To: FILE

From: Homer Picket

Date: June 17, _____ (**Year -3**)

Re: Mel Landers

        Employee #56123

Employee reported directly to me that employee committed a traffic violation for speeding (40 mph in 30 mph zone) while driving family vehicle on June 15, _____ (**Year -3**).

Homer Picket

Picket Up Delivery Services

The Big Green Transport Machine

Letter of Reprimand
Mel Landers—Employee #56123

Date: November 22, _____(Year -3)

Mel Landers
5151 Sherwood Forest Blvd.
Middleboro, Nita

Dear Mel Landers:

Thank you for meeting with me in my office today to discuss your second violation of the company's Traffic Violation Policy[1] that occurred one week ago today on November 15,_____ **(Year -3).** You committed a traffic violation for failing to come to a complete stop at a so-designated traffic sign while driving a Picket Up Delivery Services vehicle.

As I told you in our meeting, when I reviewed your employee personnel file prior to our meeting, I was made aware of the first traffic violation you committed on June 15, _____**(Year -3)** that was noted by President Homer Picket.

In regard to our meeting, I am glad that I was fully able to explain to you the company's firm policy on traffic violations that was implemented on January 1,_____ **(Year -3)**. In the future, if you have any questions regarding the traffic violations disciplinary policy, please refer to the Collective Bargaining Agreement, Article 28, and the Traffic Violation Policy, B(1) in the company's policy manual. That Policy is also posted on the company bulletin boards and on our Web site. As I related to you in our meeting, we at Picket Up Delivery Services value highly the safety of our employees and the public at large. It is for that very reason we have taken a firm stand on a safe driving record of our employees.

This letter acts as a reprimand for the second violation of PUDS' Traffic Violation Policy. A copy of this reprimand will be placed in your personnel file. While the Policy could authorize the company to suspend you for up to thirty (30) days without pay, we have chosen not to do so. I am compelled to remind you that a third traffic violation committed within five (5) years could result in your termination.

Regards,

Juliette Nelson-Picket

Juliette Nelson-Picket, Vice President
Picket Up Delivery Services

cc: Employee personnel file

[1]See Critical Work Rule Policy for drivers of PUDS' vehicles adopted January 1, _____**(Year -3)** under Article 28 B(1) of Collective Bargaining Agreement and through contract negotiations with appropriate union representatives.

METROPOLITAN NEWS

L. Marie, Publisher; John Oliver, Editor

What's Inside:

Santa and Reindeer Spotted on NASA Satellite!

Hollywood Eliminates All Animated Animal Appearances In Future Feature Films! NEMO files protest.

December 24,_____ (Year -2)

Christmas Traffic Accident Takes Its Toll!

A tragic accident took place yesterday at approximately 7:00 p.m. when community activist and business entrepreneur, Helen (who has been called "Pretty" since childhood) Darngood was struck and severely injured by a Picket Up Delivery Services van driven by Mel Landers.

The one witness who remained at the scene to be interviewed by the police was Cooper Earle, the owner and manager of Cooper, Grumble, and Green, Booksellers. Earle said that a green PUDS van ran a red light and struck Ms. Darngood while she was stepping into the crosswalk.

The driver of the delivery van, Mel Landers, spoke briefly to this reporter and said, "I was driving slowly and cautiously when I approached the intersection because of all the people on the sidewalks. I had the green light, and it turned yellow as I entered the intersection. I didn't speed up to get through, but suddenly a person stepped out in front of the van before I could stop."

Police officers at the scene declined to comment however, and no traffic citations were issued at the time this article was written.

Homer Picket, the seventy-three-year-old founder and owner of Picket Up Delivery Services said, "I was deeply saddened by the injuries to Helen Darngood and the pain it has caused her and her family, especially during this time of the year. I have every confidence in our driver, Mel Landers, who has been an exemplary employee for the last ten years and has a superb driving record." Mr. Picket said it was a tragic accident and "sometimes these things just happen and no one is at fault."

Landers is a softball coach and is involved with the Big Brother-Big Sister organizations. He is a single parent and has one child, William Landers, age twelve. Landers said it was terrible what happened and expressed deep sadness at the accident scene.

Both the Picket and Darngood companies are prominent companies in our city, and both companies have made financial and personal contributions to the growth of our community, thereby benefitting our children's educations and providing access to the art community.

Our community is saddened by the accident and the anguish it has caused Darngood's family and the employees of both companies.

Doctors at Nita State University Hospital indicated that Darngood remains in serious but stable condition. Her prognosis is uncertain at this time.

METROPOLITAN NEWS

L. Marie, Publisher; John Oliver, Editor

What's Inside:

Colorado Collie Wins 1ˢᵗ Annual Canine Snow Boarding Contest
First Long Distance Ice Skating Race in 50 Years To Be Held! Sports Section

January 15,_____ (Year -1)

BUSINESS SECTION

Three Companies Announce Major Initiatives

Over the past ten years St. Helens Worldwide Technology and Darngood Electronics Company have entered into many cooperative agreements regarding computers and computer software sales between both companies. Margaret Hanson, Acting-President and CEO of Darngood Electronics, announced that Darngood has been very happy with this relationship.

Homer Picket announced that Picket Up Delivery Services will soon be working as the transportation and delivery service nationwide for Darngood and St. Helens. The seventy-three-year-old owner and founder of Picket Up Delivery Services said this is the last big contract he will work on before he retires and turns the company over to his forty-one-year-old daughter, Juliette, who will sign the new agreement on behalf of Picket Up Delivery Services.

Picket said that over the years they have been working on a contract basis with Darngood and St. Helens, and it has been so successful that they are negotiating a national delivery contract agreement with St. Helens and Darngood.

In a related matter, St. Helens and Darngood have a major new initiative. The two companies have an agreement for Darngood to market a new computer software security system (SWATS) to protect commercial, industrial, and personal computers. Annual sales of the St. Helens's software system through advertising and on eBay has been at a rate of 75,000 units. The annual projections are expected to increase to 100,000 units per year within the next year.

The agreement between St. Helens and Darngood is for Darngood to purchase 1 million copies of SWATS, which will be selling at retail stores for $149.95. This will be an annual sale, which means good business for St. Helens, Darngood, and the community. The purchase is contingent upon St. Helens having sales of $100,000 of the product next year.

The agreement also includes the ability for purchasers of the current system to obtain updates for approximately $30 if they purchase the whole package. Negotiations were under way when Helen Darngood was injured on December 23, _____(Year -2). The negotiations, which would be very profitable for all sides, are on hold according to Hanson and Fran Degrew, CEO of St. Helens. Both sides await word on the health of Helen Darngood, who was the driving force behind the deal.

This reporter learned that the sale is also contingent upon a current lawsuit in which a small computer company in St. Paul, Nita, accused St. Helens of patent infringement, claiming that the security system being marketed by St. Helens violates the patent obtained by FINBAR Software Systems. That trial will take place in the very near future. Cal McPherson, President of FINBAR, says that they expect success as the violation is clear and obvious.

St. Helens denies there was a patent infringement and expects a complete victory in the case. In any event, St. Helens CEO Degrew states, "It will not affect the marketing and sales of the software system designed and developed by the engineers at St. Helens."

In another footnote, the President and CEO of Darngood Electronics, Helen Darngood, remains in the Nita State University Hospital. Her condition has improved somewhat, but her prognosis remains uncertain at this time. The entire community wishes Darngood the best. Homer Picket said he and the Picket Up employees continue to pray for the return of Darngood's health.

NITA CITY POLICE REPORT
DEPARTMENT OF PUBLIC SAFETY

CASE NO. 9999-0000

ACCIDENT REPORT	FIELD REPORT

Nature of Incident: **Date of Incident:**   **Location:**

Accident with Injury   *Dec. 23,____ (Year -2)*   *Intersection of Seventh St. &*
Smith Ave.

Time: *1900*

Reported by: **Date of Report:**   **Ticket Number:**

Officer R.J. Moore   *Dec. 24,_____ (Year -2)*   *None Issued*

Subject: **DOB:**   **Driver License Number:**

Mel Landers   *July 15,_____ (Year -35)*   *M-878021662323*

Subject Address:

5151 Sherwood Forest Blvd., Middleboro, Nita

Licence of Vehicle: **Year:**   **Make:**   **Color:**   **Owner:**

PKU-444   *___ (Year -5)*   *Ford*   *Green w/Red Letters   Picket Up Co.*

Injured Person: **DOB:**   **Address:**

Helen Darngood   *April 18, _____ (Year -37)*   *1330 Lakeview Lane, Nita City*

Witnesses: **Address:**   **Telephone:**

Cooper Earle   *612 MontCalm Blvd., Nita City*   *777-777-0007*

FACTS

I was dispatched at 1905 hours to the intersection of Seventh Street and Smith Avenue on the evening of December 23,_____(Year -2). On arrival at the scene of an apparent motor vehicle and pedestrian accident, I immediately radioed dispatch to make sure an EMT unit was enroute. I told the dispatcher there was one person injured. The dispatcher confirmed EMT unit was enroute and estimated arrival time within three to five minutes. I requested a backup patrol unit to assist with crowd and traffic control.

The accident scene involved one female victim (Helen Darngood) who was lying five feet from the right front tire of a Picket Up Delivery Services van. The van was stopped ten feet to the west of the crosswalk. The injured pedestrian lay five feet further to the west. I ascertained that the female victim was unconscious and breathing shallowly. Pulse rate was elevated. There were no visible external lacerations. There were no tears on the victim's clothing. There was a small amount of blood coming from the victim's right ear and a swelling starting to form above her right ear. I did not move the victim. The EMT unit arrived and proceeded to treat the victim and subsequently transported the victim to Nita State University Hospital. The backup unit arrived shortly after the EMT unit, and I began to reroute traffic and disperse the crowd that had formed.

The driver of the Picket Up Delivery van was crouching near the victim when I arrived. I asked the driver to vacate the immediate area and to stand beside my patrol car, which was on the street to the left side of the PUDS van.

When the victim was attended to by EMT medics, I proceeded to question the suspect for identification. The suspect produced a driver's license, #M-878021662323, identified as Mel Landers, date of birth July 15,_____ (Year -35), 5' 7", 140 pounds, brown eyes with an address of 5151 Sherwood Forest Blvd., Middleboro, Nita. I radioed station for wants or warrants on suspect. Wants and warrants came back negative and license was valid.

Landers readily admitted to being the driver of the delivery van. The van is not a commercial vehicle as it weighs less than 26,000 pounds and does not meet any other commercial vehicle criteria. The van's specifications were given to me by Landers.

PUDS VAN SPECIFICATIONS

Weight: curb weight (lbs): 5340 pounds.

External Dimensions:

     overall length (mm/in): 5893/232.0

     overall width (mm/in): 2014/79.3

     overall height (mm/in): 2149/84.6

     wheelbase (mm/in): 3505/138.0

     and curb to curb turning circle (mm/ft): 14630/48.0

Landers was not slurred of speech, but his eyes were a bit red, and he seemed dazed as to how the incident had occurred. Landers asked me repeatedly if the victim was going to be okay. Landers also expressed disbelief that an accident happened.

I smelled alcohol on the Landers's breath and asked if Landers had been drinking. Landers denied being drunk, but affirmed having a beer or two at a company holiday party earlier in the day this date. I performed a field sobriety test. Landers, although tentative, passed a field sobriety test. Landers was able to walk a straight line, say the alphabet, pick up coins on the pavement, stand on one foot with eyes closed and count one to ten, and touch nose with eyes closed with index finger on each hand starting with arms outstretched. I placed Landers in the back of my squad car.

Cooper Earle, owner and manager of Cooper, Grumble, and Green, Booksellers, whose place of business is one block south of the scene, was identified as a witness. After a brief conversation with the witness regarding the accident, I told Earle to go to the police station to give a formal statement. While there were many people around, Earle was the only person who came forward and admitted seeing the accident. Earle thought the driver had gone through a red light while the driver, Landers, said the light turned yellow just as the van entered the intersection. Earle indicated that there may have been another person who walked into the street at the same time as Helen Darngood, but Earle was not certain and no one else was hit or came forward as a witness.

Earle was carrying a heavy mussel pot in a wrapped box just before the accident. Earle dropped it, and we could not find it later. I found a picture of a mussel pot on the web and later at the bookstore. Earle said the mussel pot in the picture was like the one that was dropped and lost at the scene.

Picture of Mussel Pot

I took measurements of the accident scene and had the PUDS van impounded after reviewing the scene and after talking to Earle. There were no dents on the van. Landers told me that he did not see the injured person until she stepped in front of the van. Landers said the right front of the van hit the woman. Landers also was unsure if the woman had the green light. Earle was sure the woman, Helen Darngood, had the green light when she started to walk across the street. I took a picture of the stop and walk lights.

Photograph of Stop and Walk Signals

I prepared a speed and distance chart in order to estimate the speed of the van at the time of impact, but I did not calculate it because I determined not to issue a citation.

SPEED CALCULATION

- A vehicle traveling 60 miles per hour travels a distance of 88 feet per second.

- A vehicle traveling 15 miles per hour travels a distance of 22 feet per second.

- The intersection in this exercise is 66 feet wide.

- 5.5 seconds elapsed from the time the light turned yellow for Mel Landers until it turned green for Helen Darngood.

- A vehicle traveling 66 feet in 5.5 seconds will travel 12.363 feet in one second and the vehicle will be moving at the rate of 8.18 miles per hour.

I took Landers to police headquarters for an intoxilyzer test. Landers was read the *Miranda* warning, and he waived his right to remain silent. I prepared two diagrams of the accident scene—one including the van and one without the van. They are attached to this report.

State Bureau of Criminal Apprehension Toxicologist, Sing Chen, was on duty with our department and conducted the intoxilyzer tests as required by department protocol. See attached intoxilyzer tests and alcohol influence chart.

I went online and obtained a picture of the front and back of the PUDS' uniform shirt like the shirt Mel Landers was wearing.

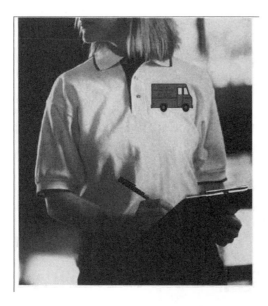 

Photographs of PUDS Uniform Shirt

Darngood v. Landers and PUDS, Plaintiff

I took a picture of downtown Nita City that evening when the stores were closed. The picture's orientation is looking north on Seventh Street from Grand Avenue.

I did not issue a citation because of conflict in testimony and lack of witnesses. I reviewed the results of the intoxilyzer test and felt that alcohol may have had some impact, but I do not feel that a criminal case can be proved beyond a reasonable doubt. In spite of the injury, this appears to be a civil matter.

Officer Signature: *R.J. Moore*

R.J. Moore

Accident Diagram with Picket Up Delivery Services Van

Accident Diagram (not to scale)
Prepared by R.J. Moore, Dec. 24, _____ (Year -2)

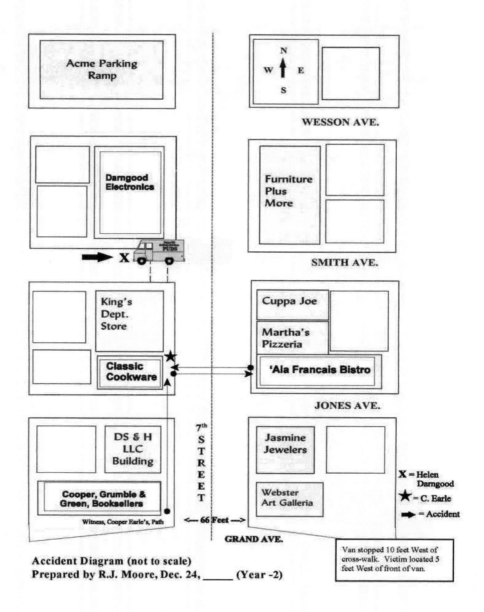

Accident Diagram (not to scale)
Prepared by R.J. Moore, Dec. 24, _____ (Year -2)

Accident Diagram Without Picket Up Delivery Services Van

Accident Diagram (not to scale)

Prepared by R.J. Moore, Dec. 24, _____ (Year -2)

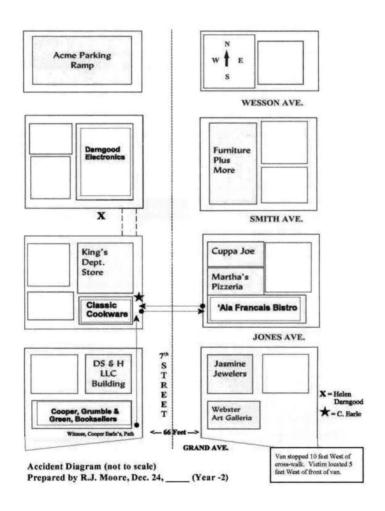

Accident Diagram (not to scale)
Prepared by R.J. Moore, Dec. 24, _____ (Year -2)

SUPPLEMENTARY TRAFFIC REPORT

No. **9999-0000**

DRIVERS LICENSE NUMBER

M-878021662323

NAME ⟁ LAST, FIRST, MIDDLE/MAIDEN

Landers, Mel

ADDRESS & CITY

5151 Sherwood Forest Blvd., Middleboro, Nita

DATE OF BIRTH	EYES	HEIGHT	WEIGHT
July 15, ____(Year -35)	BROWN	5' 7"	140

The Undersigned, being duly sworn, deposes and says that theperson named on this complaint did commit the following offense.

DATE OF OFFENSE	TIME OF OFFENSE	MAKE	MODEL
Dec. 23, ____(Year -2)	*1900*	*Ford*	*Delivery Van*

VEHICLE LICENSE PLATE/STATE YR.	COLOR
PKU - 444	*Green w/Red Lettering*

LOCATION

Intersection of Seventh Street and Smith Avenue

STATUTE/ORDINANCE   **DESCRIPTION**

Not Applicable

SPEED (over limit)   COM   CD   CO   CD   CT   CD   ACT.   CODE

____ mph in __ zone

☒ ENDANGER LIFE OR PROPERTY ☒ ACCIDENT ☐ UNSAFE CONDITIONS
☐ COMMERCIAL VEHICLE ☐ PROPERTY DAMAGE ☐ HAZARDOUS MATERIALS
   (OVER 26,000 GVW) OR BUS ☒ PERSONAL INJURY   (ANY SIZE VEHICLE)
   16 OR MORE PASSENGERS ☐ MOTORCYCLE ☐ PETTY MISDEMEANOR

NAME	BADGE #
R.J. Moore	0228

ICR NUMBER

9999-0000

REMARKS:

COMPLAINANT SIGNATURE:

R.J. Moore

ALCOHOL INFLUENCE REPORT

(Page 1 of 3)

Nita Dept. of Public Safety

Case No. __9999-0000__

Alcohol Influence Report

Date: __December 23,____(Year -2)__

<table>
<tr><td>_X_ Accident</td><td>_X_ **Driver**</td></tr>
<tr><td>__ Violation</td><td>__ Pedes.</td></tr>
<tr><td></td><td>__ Pass.</td></tr>
<tr><td></td><td>__ Other</td></tr>
</table>

NAME: __Mel Landers__

TIME: __19:46 p.m.__

DOB: __July 15,___(Year -35)__

ACTIONS OF DRIVER PRIOR TO STOP

DL: __M-878021662323__

(A) __ Weave from lane to lane

(B) __ Proceed in lane provided for oncoming car

ARRESTING OFFICER:

(C) __ Proceed off the road from his lane of traffic

__R.J. Moore__

(D) __ Make an improper turn

(E) __ Proceed at excessive / reduced speed

(F) __ Strike any gutter or other obstacles on road

BADGE: __0228__

(G) _X_ Hit or nearly hit any person or property

(H) __ Proceed contrary to traffic control device

(I) _X_ Involved in any accident

LOCATION OF INCIDENT:

(J) __ Other (explain on reverse side)

__Corner of Seventh Street and Smith Avenue__

(K) __ Road Type _X_ Two Way Street
__ Divided _ Interstate _ 2-Lane

FIELD SOBRIETY TESTS

Straight Line Walking	✓Pass	Fail
Finger to Nose	✓Pass	Fail
Say Alphabet	✓Pass	Fail
One Leg stand & count	✓Pass	Fail
Pick up coins	✓Pass	Fail

Darngood v. Landers and PUDS, Plaintiff

ALCOHOL INFLUENCE REPORT
(Page 2 of 3)

YOUR CONSTITUTIONAL RIGHTS (Time: __19:46 p.m.__)

1.   You have the right to remain silent.

2.   Anything you say can and will be used against you in a court of law.

3.   You have the right to a lawyer and to have the lawyer present while you are being questioned.

4.   If you cannot financially afford to hire a lawyer, the Court, after investigation as to your finances, will appoint a lawyer to represent you prior to any questioning if you wish one.

DO YOU UNDERSTAND THESE RIGHTS? __X__ Yes __ No

---

1.   Having these rights in mind, do you wish to answer my questions at this time?
        Yes __X__   No ___

2.   Were you driving or operating a motor vehicle? ___*Sure*___

3.   What type of vehicle were you operating? ___*The Picket Up Delivery Van*___

4.   Are you under a doctor or dentist's care? ___*No*___

5.   If so, what is your doctor or dentist's name?

6.   Are you taking any medication? ___*No*___

7.   What kind?

8.   Date/Time last taken?

9.   Dosage?

10.   Do you have diabetes? ___*No*___

11.   Medication?

12.   Date/Time last taken?

ALCOHOL INFLUENCE REPORT
(Page 3 of 3)

13. Do you have any physical disability?   ___*No*

14. Do you have any speech difficulty?   ___*No*

15. Have you been in an accident?   ___*No, never before, this is my first*

16. Did you get a bump on the head or any other injury?   ___*No*

17. What time is it?   ___*A little before 8 p.m.*

18. Where are you now?   ___*Police station*

19. Have you been drinking?   *I had some beer at the Picket Up company holiday party*

20. What did you drink?   ___*Two or three Sam Adams*

21. Where were you drinking?   ___*At the Picket Up holiday party*

22. When did you have your first drink?   ___*about 3:45 p.m.*

23. Last drink?   ___*I don't recall, I think it was about 6:30 p.m.*

24. Have you had anything to drink since the accident or arrest?   ___*No*

25. Has your consumption of alcohol affected you?   ___*No, I don't think so*

26. Your ability to drive?   ___*Absolutely not*

DEPARTMENT OF PUBLIC SAFETY
DRIVER'S LICENSE RECORD

DRIVER'S LICENSE NUMBER: ___**M-878021662323**	DRIVER'S RECORD:	1. **Speeding Citation** **(Year -3)** 2. **Failure to Stop for Semaphore** **(Year -3)**
NAME: ___**Mel Landers**	STATUS: ___**Current**	
EYES: ___**Brown**	HEIGHT: ___**5'7"**	WEIGHT: ___**140#**
ADDRESS: ___**5151 Sherwood Forest Blvd.** ___**Middleboro, Nita**	DOB: ___**July 15,** **(Year -35)**	

R.J. Moore

R.J. Moore

Darngood v. Landers and PUDS, Plaintiff

**ATTACHMENT TO
NITA CITY POLICE REPORT
NITA DEPARTMENT OF PUBLIC SAFETY
TOXICOLOGY REPORT
COVER SHEET**

Follow-Up Report by R.J. Moore

RE: Mel Landers   Cover Sheet Attachment Date: **January 5, _____(Year -1)**

CASE NO.   9999-0000

TOXICOLOGY REPORT PREPARED AND SIGNED BY: *Sing Chen*

                                                  **Sing Chen, Toxicologist
                                                  Nita Department of Public Safety**

DATE OF TESTING: December 23,   (Year -2)

**Attached find the results of the intoxilyzer testing that was performed on subject:
      Mel Landers
      5151 Sherwood Forest Blvd., Middleboro, Nita
      Nita Driver's License No. #M-878021662323**

Testing was completed at: 2030 hours, December 23, _____(Year -2).

Attached are:
      1.   **Intoxilyzer Test Record #530109,**
      2.   **Intoxilyzer Log, and**
      3.   **Alcohol Impairment Charts.**

Signed by:

R.J. Moore

R.J. Moore

Date: January 5, _____ **(Year -1)**

Intoxilyzer Test Record
(Page 1 of 3)

530109

INTOXILYZER TEST RECORD
MODEL 5000   SN 64-000241

Date: __December 23,   (Year -2)__

	TEST	AC	TIME
01	DIAGNOSTIC OK	45+5	DEG C
02	AIR BLANK	.000	20:26
03	SUBJECT TEST	.059	20:27
04	REPLICATE TEST	.059	20:27
05	AIR BLANK	.000	20:28
06	CAL. STD.	.080	20:28
07	REPLICATE TEST	.082	20:28
08	AIR BLANK	.000	20:29
09	SUBJECT TEST	.061	20:29
10	REPLICATE TEST	.061	20:29
11	AIR BLANK	.000	20:30
12	BREATH CORRELATION =		97%
13	REPORTED VALUE	.059	20:30

DO NOT WRITE ABOVE LINE

Purpose
of test: [X] Traffic   [ ] Other

Subject: ___*Mel Landers*___

DOB *July 15,   (Year -35)*

Operator: *Sing Chen*

Dept: *Nita Department of Public Safety*

Certificate   Simulator
                               Solution
Number: __*3330*__   Number: __*91036*__

Subject has been under observation for 15-20 minutes by __RM__

Record simulator temperature (33.8°--34.2°C) *34.0°* °C

REMARKS: *Breath tube warm to touch*
               Subject gave 2 good strong breaths

OPERATOR'S

SIGNATURE: *Sing Chen*   *#3331*

REFERENCE

NUMBER: __*9105-0402*__
FORM PS-50591-01

Darngood v. Landers and PUDS, Plaintiff

Intoxilyzer Test Record
(Page 2 of 3)

PART 1 — ORIGINAL
INTOXILYZER LOG

The Intoxilyzer Log keeps a record of every breath test taken on that instrument. The test number, test date, simulator tests, subject results and operator certification number are all recorded. The simulator solution needs to be changed after a page is completely filled out or at the end of each month. The purpose of the log is to keep a record of the performance of each machine, to know when the solution needs to be changed, and to serve as an indicator if the instrument is malfunctioning.

See next page for the log.

Intoxilyzer Test Record
(Page 3 of 3)

INTOXILYZER LOG

PS-50592-01

DEPARTMENT ___Nita Department of Public Safety___   INTOXILYZER   Serial No. __0241__

Simulator Solution Number __91032__

SIMULATOR SOLUTION MUST BE CHANGED BEFORE THE FIRST SUBJECT TEST OF THE MONTH OR AT THE END OF THE LOG SHEET, WHICHEVER OCCURS FIRST.

TEST RECORD NUMBER	DATE OF TEST and TIME	SUBJECT	SUBJECT RESULTS		SIMULATOR RESULTS		OPERATOR CERT. NO.
530179		SIMULATOR			*.103*		*2007*
	December (Year-2)	SIMULATOR			*.109*		
		SIMULATOR			*.111*		
530101	Dec 22/1910	Marcia Ruhr	.223	.227	.109	.110	2808
530102	Dec 22/2100	Lorence Sherman	.136	.140	.115	.116	2007
530103	Dec 22/2330	Joe Crockett	.099	.100	.117	.118	3331
530104	Dec 23/1520	Andrew Summers	.261	.265	.112	.112	1442
530105	Dec 23/1800	Leroy Duchesne	.124	.126	.108	.109	3267
530106	Dec 23/1920	Frederick Moullette	.100	.102	.106	.108	3267
530107	**Dec 23/2030**	**Mel Landers**	**.059**	**.061**	**.080**	**.082**	**3331**
530108	Dec 23/2215	Stephen Larsin	.090	.092	.110	.111	3331
530109	Dec 23/2330	Tracy Dobbs	.139	.141	.110	.112	3336

Darngood v. Landers and PUDS, Plaintiff

Alcohol Impairment Charts* (Page 1 of 2)

Alcohol affects individuals differently. Blood alcohol level may be affected by age, gender, physical condition, amount of food consumed and any drugs or medication. In addition, different drinks may contain different amounts of alcohol. For purposes of this guide, "one drink" is equal to 1.5 oz. of 80 proof liquor, 12 oz. of regular beer, or 5 oz. of table wine.

A woman drinking an equal amount of alcohol in the same period of time as a man of an equivalent weight may have a higher blood alcohol level than the man. Some states have set .08% Blood Alcohol Concentration (BAC) as the legal limit for Driving Under the Influence. For commercial drivers, a BAC of .04% can result in a DUI conviction nationwide. Impairment begins with a first drink.

MEN									
Approximate Blood Alcohol Percentage									
Drinks	**Body Weight in Pounds**								
	100	120	140	160	180	200	220	240	
0	.00	.00	.00	.00	.00	.00	.00	.00	**Only Safe Driving Limit**
1	.04	.03	.03	.02	.02	.02	.02	.02	Impairment begins
2	.08	.06	.05	.05	.04	.04	.03	.03	Driving Skills Affected ------- Possible Criminal Penalties
3	.11	.09	.08	.07	.06	.06	.05	.05	
4	.15	.12	.11	.09	.08	.08	.07	.06	
5	.19	.16	.13	.12	.11	.09	.09	.08	
6	.23	.19	.16	.14	.13	.11	.10	.09	
7	.26	.22	.19	.16	.15	.13	.12	.11	
8	.30	.25	.21	.19	.17	.15	.14	.13	Legally Intoxicated ----- Criminal Penalties
9	.34	.28	.24	.21	.19	.17	.15	.14	
10	.38	.31	.27	.23	.21	.19	.17	.16	
Your body can get rid of one drink per hour. One drink is 1.5 oz. of 80 proof liquor, 12 oz. of beer, or 5 oz. of table wine									

WOMEN										
Approximate Blood Alcohol Percentage										
Drinks	**Body Weight in Pounds**									
	90	100	120	140	160	180	200	220	240	
0	.00	.00	.00	.00	.00	.00	.00	.00	.00	**Only Safe Driving Limit**
1	.05	.05	.04	.03	.03	.03	.02	.02	.02	Impairment begins
2	.10	.09	.08	.07	.06	.05	.05	.04	.04	Driving Skills Affected ------- Possible Criminal Penalties
3	.15	.14	.11	.10	.09	.08	.07	.06	.06	
4	.20	.18	.15	.13	.11	.10	.09	.08	.08	
5	.25	.23	.19	.16	.14	.13	.11	.10	.09	
6	.30	.27	.23	.19	.17	.15	.14	.12	.11	Legally Intoxicated ----- Criminal Penalties
7	.35	.32	.27	.23	.20	.18	.16	.14	.13	
8	.40	.36	.30	.26	.23	.20	.18	.17	.15	
9	.45	.41	.34	.29	.26	.23	.20	.19	.17	
10	.51	.45	.38	.32	.28	.25	.23	.21	19	
Your body can get rid of one drink per hour. One drink is 1.25 oz. of 80 proof liquor, 12 oz. of beer, or 5 oz. of table wine										

* Data supplied by the Pennsylvania Liquor Control Board - http://www.health.org/nongovpubs/bac-chart/

Alcohol Impairment Charts

(Page 2 of 2)

Driving Under the Influence*

*From Dui.com

Blood Alcohol Content	Effects
.04	Speech impairment
.04	Commercial impairment levels
.05	Legal presumption starts
.08	Legal definition of under the influence
.10	Accident curve rises to 6 X's more likely
.14	20 X's more likely to have accident
.16	35 X's more likely to have accident
.20	Stumbling
.30	Vomiting, passing out
.40	Coma
.50	Coma, Death
.60	Death

Rate of Absorption
1. 60–90 minutes all alcohol absorbed
2. Empty stomach 50% in 15 minutes
3. Full stomach 50% in 40 minutes
4. Mixed drinks more carbon dioxide
5. Health of stomach lining
6. Small intestines absorb 80% of alcohol
7. Stomach 20% absorption
8. Males 58% water in blood
9. Females 48% water in blood

Darngood v. Landers and PUDS, Plaintiff

Darngood Electronics
700 Smith Avenue
Nita City, Nita
A leader in electronics, household appliances and music
We're Better Than Good, We're Darngood!

June 10, _____ **(Year -1)**

Board of Directors
Darngood Electronics
700 Smith Avenue
Nita City, Nita

Dear Board of Directors:

It is with deep regret that I must resign my position as President and Chief Executive Officer of Darngood Electronics. It has been my and my father's dream to build Darngood Electronics into a Fortune 500 international company. Since my unfortunate accident last December, I have not been able to function with the same level of intellect and energy that I once had. My doctors have informed me that there will be no improvement. I may suffer seizures and other illnesses. While my medications may control these, it affects me to such an extent that I cannot serve the company as I once did. Unfortunately, I did not have a succession plan in place. I had hoped to achieve this, but I was busy with other matters.

I have discussed this matter with Margaret Hanson, and she is aware of some of the plans I had hoped to put in place. I suggest that you appoint her as Acting Chief Executive Officer and Acting President of Darngood Electronics. She will do well for all of us. As you begin a new plan for management, I am sure you will take great care in selecting the right management team. In any event, I hope you will consider Margaret as you conduct your thorough analysis of candidates for this vital role in the company.

Sincerely,

Helen Darngood

Helen Darngood

PLEADINGS

SUMMONS, COMPLAINT, AND ANSWER

STATE OF NITA

COUNTY OF DARROW

DISTRICT COURT

SECOND JUDICIAL DISTRICT

Court File No. 3543

HELEN DARNGOOD

Plaintiff,

v.

MEL LANDERS, AN INDIVIDUAL,

AND PICKET UP DELIVERY SERVICES,

A NITA CORPORATION

Defendants.

SUMMONS

THE STATE OF NITA TO THE ABOVE-NAMED DEFENDANTS:

YOU ARE HEREBY SUMMONED and required to serve upon Plaintiff's attorneys an Answer to the Complaint, which is herewith served upon you, within twenty (20) days after service of the Summons upon you, exclusive of the day of service. If you fail to do so, judgment by default will be taken against you for the relief demanded in the Complaint.

Date:_____ **(First Monday, Month -5)**

R.W. Fingal

R.W. Fingal
ATTORNEY FOR PLAINTIFF

STATE OF NITA

COUNTY OF DARROW

DISTRICT COURT

SECOND JUDICIAL DISTRICT

Court File No. 3543

HELEN DARNGOOD

Plaintiff,

v.

COMPLAINT

MEL LANDERS, AN INDIVIDUAL,

AND PICKET UP DELIVERY SERVICES,

A NITA CORPORATION

Defendants.

Plaintiff Helen Darngood for her complaint against Defendants Mel Landers and Picket Up Delivery Services states and alleges as follows:

I.

At all times relevant to this action Plaintiff Helen Darngood has been and is a resident of the County of Darrow, State of Nita and currently resides at 1330 Lakeview Lane, Nita City, Nita.

II.

At all times relevant to this action Defendant Mel Landers has been and is a resident of the County of Darrow, State of Nita and currently resides at 5151 Sherwood Forest Blvd., Middleboro, Nita.

III.

At all times relevant to this action Defendant Picket Up Delivery Services has been and is a Nita Corporation located at 1965 Industrial Blvd., Nita City, Nita.

IV.

On or about December 23, _____**(Year -2)**, at approximately 7:00 p.m., a Picket-Up Delivery Services van driven by Defendant Mel Landers struck Plaintiff Helen Darngood at the corner of Seventh Street and Smith Avenue in Nita City, Nita.

V.

As a direct result of this accident Plaintiff has suffered numerous medical injuries. Because of these injuries Plaintiff has incurred past medical expenses and will also continue to require future medical care thereby incurring future medical expenses.

VI.

As a direct result of being struck by the vehicle operated by Defendant, Plaintiff has in the past and will in the future suffer a loss of earnings and loss of earning capacity.

COUNT I

NEGLIGENCE

VII.

Defendant Landers acted within the scope of employment while working as an employee of Picket Up Delivery Services when the Picket Up Delivery Services van struck Plaintiff Helen Darngood.

VIII.

Defendant Landers acted negligently when driving Defendant Picket Up Delivery Services's vehicle in a manner that placed Plaintiff and other pedestrians in danger and subsequently striking Plaintiff with the vehicle Defendant Landers was operating.

IX.

Defendant Landers's negligent behavior in driving the vehicle was the direct cause of Plaintiff's severe and numerous injuries.

X.

As a direct result of Defendant Landers's carelessness and negligence, Plaintiff has incurred, and will incur in the future, medical expenses, including medical attention and treatment, hospitalization, medicines and drugs in an amount to be determined.

COUNT II

RESPONDEAT SUPERIOR

(Defendant Picket Up Delivery Services)

XI.

Defendant Picket Up Delivery Services owed Plaintiff a duty of care that Picket Up Delivery Services employee, Mel Landers, would drive carefully and avoid hitting pedestrians, such as Plaintiff, with the Picket Up Delivery Services vehicle.

XII.

Defendant Picket Up Delivery Services breached this duty of care when Defendant Mel Landers negligently drove Defendant Picket Up Delivery Services's vehicle in a manner that placed Plaintiff and other pedestrians in danger and subsequently striking Plaintiff.

Darngood v. Landers and PUDS, Plaintiff

XIII.

Defendant Mel Landers was acting within the scope of employment as an employee of Defendant Picket Up Delivery Services at the time of the accident.

XIV.

As a result of Defendant Landers's behavior in the course and scope of Defendant Landers's employment, Defendant Picket Up Delivery Services is liable under the doctrine of respondeat superior for the actions of its employee, Defendant Mel Landers.

WHEREFORE Plaintiff prays for the following relief:

1. Awarding Plaintiff the past medical expenses in an amount to be determined.

2. Awarding Plaintiff all future medical expenses in an amount to be determined.

3. Awarding Plaintiff compensation for loss of earnings in an amount to be determined.

4. Awarding Plaintiff compensation for future lost earning capacity in an amount to be determined.

5. Awarding Plaintiff any and all other remedies the court so deems just.

Date:_____ **(First Monday, Month - 5)**   *R.W. Fingal*

R.W. Fingal
ATTORNEY FOR PLAINTIFF

STATE OF NITA

COUNTY OF DARROW

DISTRICT COURT

SECOND JUDICIAL DISTRICT

Court File No. 3543

HELEN DARNGOOD

Plaintiff,

v.

MEL LANDERS, AN INDIVIDUAL,

AND PICKET UP DELIVERY SERVICES,

A NITA CORPORATION

Defendants.

DEFENDANTS' ANSWER

TO COMPLAINT

ANSWER

The Defendants state the following as Answer to Plaintiff's complaint:

1. Admits each and every allegation in paragraphs I through IV, VII, XI, and XIII.

2. In answer to the allegations in paragraphs VIII through X, XII, and XIV, Defendants are informed and believe that the allegations are untrue, and based on that information and belief denies the truth of each and every allegation in the paragraphs.

3. In answer to the allegations in paragraphs V and VI, Defendants allege that Defendants have no information and belief on the subject sufficient to form an answer, and based on that lack of information and belief, denies each and every allegation.

FIRST AFFIRMATIVE DEFENSE

As a first affirmative defense, Defendants allege Plaintiff was guilty of contributory negligence in that Plaintiff failed to keep a proper lookout for automobiles then on the roadway. Plaintiff failed to exercise ordinary care on Plaintiff's own behalf with regard to the incident alleged in Plaintiff's complaint in the following respects:

a. Plaintiff failed to keep an adequate lookout for vehicles using the roadway; and

b. Plaintiff failed to undertake proper acts to avoid or evade the claimed injury.

The preceding acts or omissions of Plaintiff were negligent, and Plaintiff's negligence was greater than that of Defendants, if any. Accordingly, Plaintiff should not recover from Defendants, or Plaintiff's damages should be proportionately reduced by an amount commensurate with Plaintiff's negligence.

SECOND AFFIRMATIVE DEFENSE

As a second affirmative defense Defendants allege any injuries Plaintiff may have sustained were caused by Plaintiff's own carelessness and negligence directly contributing thereto in failing to exercise care for Plaintiff's own safety. Plaintiff was guilty of contributory negligence in that Plaintiff attempted to cross the street at Seventh Street and Smith Avenue at a time that was unsafe. Plaintiff darted from the sidewalk directly into the path of Defendants' delivery van and by Plaintiff's actions contributed to Plaintiff's injuries.

THIRD AFFIRMATIVE DEFENSE

As a third affirmative defense, Defendants allege that if Plaintiff was not guilty of contributory negligence that directly and proximately caused the injury, then the injury directly and proximately resulted from an unavoidable accident, in that Defendant driver did not and could not, by the exercise of ordinary care, see Plaintiff or anticipate Plaintiff's presence or position of peril in the street as alleged by Plaintiff.

Defendants ask the Court that:

1. Plaintiff's complaint be dismissed with prejudice and that Plaintiff take nothing;

2. Defendants be awarded the costs of this action; and

3. Defendants be granted such other and further relief as the court deems proper.

Date:_____**(Third Monday, Month - 5)**   *Scott Phillips*

Scott Phillips
ATTORNEY FOR DEFENDANTS

STATEMENTS / DEPOSITIONS

DEPOSITION OF HELEN DARNGOOD

Date: _____ **(Third Thursday, Month -2)**

Helen (nickname "Pretty") Darngood

Age: 37 years old, born April 18, _____**(Year -37)**.

Married: Married, George Carpenter, age 43.

Three children: daughters: Krista, age 12; Kari, age 11; and son: James, age 8.

Education: Stanford University, BA in English and Communications,_____ **(Year -15)**.

Nita State University, MBA, _____**(Year -12)**.

Employment:

- Operations Assistant, Darngood Electronics, _____**(Year -12)** to _____**(Year -10)**.
- Operations Manager, Darngood Electronics, _____**(Year -10)** to _____**(Year -8)**.
- Vice President Operations and Business Manager, Darngood Electronics, _____**(Year -8) to** _____**(Year -5)**.
- President and CEO of Darngood Electronics, _____**(Year -5)** to June 10, _____**(Year -1)**.

1   I am a very energetic person. I walk fast. On the day I was hurt, I remember the walk signal and light
2 turning green. The picture of the street scene is how it looked at night. As the walk signal came on and
3 the light turned green, I started across the street. The picture of the stop and walk signals is accurate. I
4 had taken two steps, about six feet, when a van came out of nowhere. I was only aware of the van just
5 before it hit me. There may have been another person who started into the street when I did, but I am not
6 sure of that. I have no other memory of what happened. I was on my way to the Classic Cookware Store
7 to get three bottles of olive oil for Christmas gifts. The diagram of the area where I was hit is accurate
8 although not to scale. I do not know where Cooper Earle was at the time of the accident. I do not know
9 anything about the size of the van or where anyone else was. There were a lot of people on the street. As
10 I was walking to the intersection before the accident, I was thinking about taking a few days off to spend
11 more time with my family. I had been working very hard, and I needed a break. I am sure my family
12 would have enjoyed me being at home more.

13   I have no memory of my treatment for the next week afterwards. Before the accident I was a hard-
14 charging executive. My work and my family were my life. However, on balance, I probably spent too
15 much time on my job and did not see my husband or kids as much as I should have. We built Darngood
16 Electronics into something that my father and I had dreamed of, and I really worked all the time. It was
17 good that my husband had a flexible job and could be there for the kids. I missed a lot of school
18 conferences and school activities.

19   I was active in the community and am on a number of Boards of Directors of charitable institutions,
20 such as the Northern Opera Company, the American Red Cross, the Nita Historical Society, and I serve
21 on the Humanities and Arts Section of the Nita City Chamber of Commerce. Since my accident, I do not
22 have the energy to serve on any boards. My personality has changed, and I have had to slow down.

23   Our family is wealthy. My husband has a very good job, and I own substantial stock and other
24 investments. I was a hard-charging person. I walked too fast. I didn't take time to eat. I drank a lot of
25 coffee. I admit that I was impatient and that oftentimes I was the first person across the street, although
26 I don't recall ever not waiting for a green light as I wanted to set a good example for my kids. I explained
27 to my children how important it is to pay attention and obey all the rules when walking at an intersection.
28 I always said to look both ways to be safe. I know the driving rules and have driven from the time I was

1 sixteen. I know that vehicles can enter an intersection on a yellow light and have done so myself. I know
2 a pedestrian should be careful because drivers are not always careful themselves. I am always careful.

3   Perhaps this is a good thing that happened to me, as I will have more time to spend with George and
4 the children. I can't think as fast as I used to because of the medications. I do not have any pain, but I am
5 fearful of having a seizure. Although I try to see the bright side, I get depressed, and I'm not as much fun
6 as I used to be. I don't joke and laugh with the kids although I think it is clear to them how much I love
7 them. I am now able to spend more time with them at school and in their hobbies. I am still able to help
8 them with their homework and other things, but I worry that I will not be able to help them with more
9 complex subjects when they get older. I cannot add or subtract like I used to do. I feel like my mind is
10 sort of cloudy and muddled. I used to play cribbage with George, but I no longer play because I can't
11 keep track of the cards.

12   I am afraid of having a seizure. Doctor Strickland told me if I stopped taking medication I can have
13 a seizure at any time. The doctor told me that a grand mal seizure can cause unconsciousness, loss of
14 bladder and bowel control, and other injuries such as bruising and possible biting of my tongue. I have
15 been told while there is a slight possibility I could have a seizure, I should not experience seizures while
16 taking medication. I do not remember what happens to me when my medication doesn't work. I have
17 been told that I act inappropriately. That is not like me. I know that I embarrass my husband and my
18 children. I am really afraid of having a seizure. I know it might happen some day and that would be
19 devastating for my family. I live in fear all the time. I cannot drive a car now, and that is depressing. I
20 am trying to make the best of everything, but I get very depressed sometimes, particularly when I get
21 tired. I feel terrible that I am not the same person and will not be a good mother or wife. I often feel there
22 is no hope, but I am doing the best I can.

23   Before the accident I was the President of Darngood Electronics. I earned a yearly salary of
24 $200,000. While I could have justified a higher salary based on how much Darngood Electronics was
25 growing and how well the company was doing, I chose to put this money into development. The job was
26 very important to me. Next to my family, it was the most important thing to me. I loved building a
27 company and following in my father's footsteps. I made the decision on June 10, _____**(Year -1)** to
28 resign from the company. I wrote the letter. I resigned because I could no longer perform my job.

    I have read the foregoing transcript of my deposition, given on the date below, and find it is a true
and accurate representation of my testimony.

Signed this _____**(Third Thursday, Month -2)**

Helen Darngood

Helen Darngood

Reported by : *Patric Kinski*

Patric Kinski, RMR (Registered Merit Reporter), CRR (Certified Realtime Reporter)

        Darngood v. Landers and PUDS, Plaintiff

DEPOSITION OF COOPER EARLE

Date: _____ **(Second Wednesday, Month -2)**

Cooper Earle
Age: 37 years old, born November 10, _____**(Year -37)**.
Married: Married. Two daughters, ages 10 and 8.
Education: Harvard University, BA. Majoring in Classic Literature, Minor in Art and Music, _____**(Year -15)**.
Nita State University, MBA in Business Management, _____**(Year -12)**.
Employment: Store Owner / Manager for Cooper, Grumble, and Green, Booksellers _____**(Year -11) to present**.

1   I am thirty-seven years old and the owner of Cooper, Grumble, and Green, Booksellers [Fine Books,
2   Fine Art, Fine Maps, Fine Music] on Seventh Street. My partners are Clive Grumble and Lillian Green.
3   Cooper, Grumble, and Green, Booksellers, is a specialty book, art, and music store. We cannot compete
4   with the chain book stores, so in order to be successful we carved out a specialty niche for ourselves. We
5   are very successful. In order to fit our specialty image, I always dress in conservative classic clothing at
6   work. This clothing is a "sort of" uniform to establish our branding and market niche. We built our store
7   to fit an image of an English club. We have many small rooms that are paneled in wood. I had a friend
8   make the paneling, and many rooms have gas fireplaces that look like they burn coal. The fireplaces are
9   for effect and do not give off much heat. There are lots of leather wing chairs and antiques. We sell good
10 antique furniture and reproductions. The art work is hung on the walls and occasionally placed
11 strategically on the floor. All the art and furniture are for sale as well as the books and music. Some
12 rooms are designed solely for listening to music. We offer coffee, tea, cookies, and scones at no charge
13 to customers. Cooper, Grumble, and Green, Booksellers's staff always dress in conservative classic
14 clothing as well. Many of our staff are mature people who understand good literature, fine art, and
15 classical music. While I may appear somewhat geekish, I played rugby at Harvard and am quite active
16 as a runner. I compete in marathons with my spouse, who is also a runner.
17   I worked very hard during the week of the twenty-third to get ready for the holidays. December is
18 the most important time of the year for retail sales. In addition, I've had a difficult time trying to
19 adequately staff the store for the past month. We have to hire staff carefully to fit our image. I have been
20 filling in for numerous ill and/or absent sales people. I was tired at the end of the day.
21   After leaving work, at about 6:00 p.m., I walked up to the Classic Cookware store on the corner of
22 Seventh and Jones to buy a lovely new ceramic and cast-iron pot to cook mussels for my spouse. We had
23 been doing some creative cooking, and there was a new pot that just came out on the market. I saw the
24 pot advertised at the Classic Cookware store. I purchased the mussel pot and asked the clerk to wrap it
25 for me. I'm not particularly good at wrapping. I then went across the street to 'Ala Francais Bistro to have
26 a glass of wine with a friend. I had one glass of white Chardonnay that helped me relax from the stress
27 of a busy day. I was not intoxicated.
28   I went back to the Classic Cookware store to pick up the mussel pot and began to travel north on
29 Seventh Street, two blocks or so, to my parking ramp. The picture of the mussel pot looks like the pot
30 I purchased. The picture of the downtown area is accurate. I walk the same route every day. I was excited
31 about getting home and seeing my children and my spouse. This is a very important time for me with my
32 family. I planned to have dinner with my family. My spouse had the day off and was planning to cook
33 dinner. I was looking forward to having dinner, tucking my kids in bed, taking a hot shower, getting in
34 my pajamas and robe, and sitting in front of the gas fireplace with a good book. Even though I manage
35 a book store, I still like what I call "No-Brainer Novels." I read them when I relax or travel. I had a new
36 Walter Mosley novel to read. I was looking forward to relaxing and then giving my holiday present to
37 my spouse.

1   On my way to the parking garage, I noticed that the street was busy and there were lots of people out
2   on it. It was pretty cold. Everybody was downtown for the Hollidazzle parade, which starts at about 7:00.
3   I was glad to be going home before the parade so I could beat the traffic. There were lots of cars and
4   buses on the streets. That's typical for that time of day. I am a detail-oriented kind of person, and when
5   I got about sixty feet from the intersection of Seventh and Smith, my attention was drawn to a bright
6   green Picket Up Delivery Services van entering the intersection going fast from right to left—east to
7   west. I thought, "Wow, somebody is going to get hit!" I saw the light turn green for north and south
8   bound traffic, and it must have turned red for the van. I cannot say for certain where the van was when
9   the light turned green and the walk sign came on for Helen Darngood—I know for certain that she had
10   the green light. I did see the walk signal for the pedestrians across the street from me. The picture of the
11   walk and stop signals is accurate. I think the van sped up as it entered the intersection. The van was going
12   too fast, maybe even twenty miles per hour. I saw the van cross the intersection. I did not recognize Helen
13   Darngood until I ran up to her after she was hit. I think there was another person who tried to walk into
14   the crosswalk when she did, but I am not one hundred percent positive. The other person must have
15   stepped back because Helen was the only person who was hit by the Picket Up van, which was driving
16   fast through the intersection. The diagram of the intersection and where I was and had been before is
17   accurate although not to scale. The van looks bigger on the diagram than it really is, but it is the same
18   color and shows about where the van and Helen ended up after the accident. The accident diagram
19   without the van is also accurate but not to scale. I dropped the package with the mussel pot that I was
20   carrying when I ran to Helen Darngood. After the ambulance left I tried to find the box, but someone
21   must have taken it.

22   I have known Helen Darngood for nearly fifteen years. I had some classes with her in the MBA
23   program at Nita State University. In the past she purchased some books, a few CDs, and a painting from
24   Cooper, Grumble, and Green, Booksellers. I do not know her well. She was an impulsive shopper. She
25   was always in a hurry. She would pop into the store, look around, make a purchase, and pop out. She
26   purchased books on American history, and I know recently she was studying the genealogy of the
27   founders of Nita. We have been in some of the same civic groups together. We are not close friends, but
28   rather social acquaintances. Helen is a very high energy person, always on the move, walking fast, a
29   president of a company, and a superb member of our community. It does not surprise me that she was the
30   first person off the curb with the walk signal. I ran to her and made sure she didn't move. She was not
31   conscious. I yelled for someone to call 911. I did not see any rips in her clothing. The van did not have
32   any damage. She was hit by the front right of the van. It is terrible what happened to her. A person knelt
33   beside Helen just as I ran up. The person was wearing a PUDS uniform, just like in the picture. The
34   person said, "Gosh, where did she come from?" I did not answer, and we both waited with her until the
35   ambulance arrived a few minutes later.

36   Picket Up Delivery Services often delivers shipments of books to my store, but I don't know the
37   driver of the van that hit Helen. I'm no medical expert, but it looked like the driver was in shock before
38   the police got there.

39   I was the only person who stayed around to talk to the police officer after the ambulance took Helen
40   away. I suppose the others did not want to get involved this close to Christmas.

Darngood v. Landers and PUDS, Plaintiff

I have read the foregoing transcript of my deposition, given on the date below, and find it is a true and accurate representation of my testimony.

Signed this _____**(Second Wednesday, Month -2)**

Cooper Earle

Cooper Earle

Reported by : *Patric Kinski*

Patric Kinski, RMR (Registered Merit Reporter), CRR (Certified Realtime Reporter)

DEPOSITION OF GEORGE CARPENTER

Date: _____ **(Third Friday, Month -2)**

George Carpenter

Age: 43 years old, born February 28, _____ **(Year -43)**.

Married: Married, Helen Darngood.

Three children: daughters: Krista, age 12; Kari, age 11; and son: James, age 8.

Education: Louisiana State University, School of Medicine, MD _____ **(Year -10)**.

Employment:

- Psychiatrist and tenured professor in Department of Psychiatry at Nita State University.

1 Helen's personality has changed since the accident. She is not as much fun as she used to be, and yet,
2 she seems to have slowed down and become more thoughtful. Her great love for her family is coming
3 forward. She used to be so involved with her work and her other commitments that she did not have as
4 much time for us as she does now. We understood that she had so much to give, and it is a great loss to
5 the community and Darngood Electronics because she can no longer be the person she was. We are
6 learning to love this new person as much we loved the old Helen.

7 It has been difficult for all of us. Helen does get depressed now and again because she remembers
8 how she used to be. The children and I encourage her all the time. Our relationship has struggled since
9 the accident. That is not to say we didn't have our struggles before, they are just different. Helen can't
10 keep track of numbers like she used to. We don't play cribbage anymore. She worries about being able
11 to help the children with school work as they get older. She doesn't sleep well anymore. Because she
12 can't drive, it has become more complex for us with the children and their activities. We all worry about
13 the possible seizures, and Helen describes her mind as cloudy and muddled. Helen is doing her best, but
14 sometimes she feels hopeless. Helen and I have been told by Doctor Strickland that if she stops taking
15 her anticonvulsant medication she could have a seizure at any time. The doctor told us that a grand mal
16 seizure can cause unconsciousness, loss of bladder and bowel control, and other injuries such as bruising
17 and possible biting of her tongue. We have been told while there is a slight possibility Helen could have
18 a seizure, she should not experience seizures while taking medication.

19 We do our best now to take it day-by-day. We anticipate there will be no changes in Helen's
20 condition and so we are learning to build a new life.

I have read the foregoing transcript of my deposition, given on the date below, and find it is a true and accurate representation of my testimony.

Signed this _____ **(Third Friday, Month -2)**

George Carpenter

George Carpenter

Reported by : *Patric Kinski*

Patric Kinski, RMR (Registered Merit Reporter), CRR (Certified Realtime Reporter)

DEPOSITION OF MARGARET HANSON

Date: _____ **(Third Wednesday, Month -2)**

Margaret Hanson

Age: 52 years old, born May 12, _____ **(Year -52)**.

Married: Divorced. One son, Sam, age 32. Two grandsons, ages 6 and 5.

Education: Nita State University, BA in Economics.

Employment:

- Vice President of Darngood Electronics, _____ **(Year -10) to** _____ **(Year -1)**.
- Acting President and CEO of Darngood Electronics, June 15, _____ **(Year -1) to present**.

1   Before her injury, Helen Darngood was the driving force behind Darngood Electronics. She built the
2   company since her father's death and was entering into negotiations with other companies such as St.
3   Helens Worldwide Technology and the Picket Up Delivery Services—both of which are excellent
4   companies.

5   The contract with St. Helens concerned the sale of a new computer security system. Helen and I
6   worked together with Fran Degrew, the President of St. Helens, toward exclusively marketing St. Helens
7   products both in this country and eventually overseas. We anticipated that the security system products
8   alone would mean a net revenue of at least $10 million dollars a year for Darngood Electronics for the
9   next ten years. This project is on hold while we sort out a line of succession for Helen and put together
10 a new management team. Helen was in charge of almost all aspects of Darngood Electronics; although
11 she and I worked very closely together, it was under her direction that our management team was
12 succeeding.

13 Helen tried to come back to work after the accident, but she was not the same person. She was not
14 able to think clearly and struggled to make decisions. She took a long time to figure things out. Her mind
15 was in slow motion. Helen seemed to work hard to be positive, but we could see she was having a rough
16 time. She talked to me about it on a number of occasions and told me she knew she could not do the job
17 and would only hurt the company. I told her to take more time and maybe things would get better.
18 However, she told me that with the medication she had to take to prevent seizures, she would never be
19 the same. She also said that even with medication it was possible, though not likely, she could have
20 another seizure, and that was of great concern to her.

21 I was not at all surprised when she sent the letter of resignation. Helen is a wonderful person, and we
22 are all very sad for her and her family.

23 We hope that our company will continue to go forward without Helen; however, substantial changes
24 are predictable. We will have to demonstrate to Fran Degrew and St. Helens Worldwide Technology that
25 Darngood Electronics will be able to carry out its plans. President Degrew has informed me that St.
26 Helens is in discussions with another retailer. I have been informed that we will have to demonstrate that
27 we can achieve what we predicted. While the loss of St. Helens' business will be a blow, it will only slow
28 our growth.

1   The relationship we had with Picket Up Delivery Services has changed since the accident. We are
2   examining whether Darngood Electronics can be involved in the lawsuit against Picket Up Delivery
3   Services and are consulting with our lawyers.

4   Helen was highly motivated and energetic. It is clear that she is not the same person and cannot
5   function at the same level in the company. While we would welcome her return, none of us believes it
6   would be good for her or the company to work with us unless she gets better. We reluctantly accepted
7   her letter of resignation. Helen was a hard-charger. I always found it difficult to keep up with her while
8   she was walking, and she'd be the first to get to her destination. And although I never saw her drive her
9   car too fast or go against a red light, she was the first to move when a light turned green or when she
10   could move forward.

      I have read the foregoing transcript of my deposition, given on the date below, and find it is a true
and accurate representation of my testimony.

Signed this _____**(Third Wednesday, Month -2)**

Margaret Hanson

Margaret Hanson

Reported by : *Patric Kinski*

Patric Kinski, RMR (Registered Merit Reporter), CRR (Certified Realtime Reporter)

                                            Darngood v. Landers and PUDS, Plaintiff

DEPOSITION OF MEL LANDERS

Date_____(**Second Thursday, Month -2**)

Mel Landers

Age: 35 years old, born July 15, _____**(Year -35)**.

Married: Widowed. One son, William, age 12.

Education: Nita High School, _____**(Year -17)**.

Nita State University, Junior status, currently enrolled in evening classes working toward BA in Business.

Employment:

- U.S. Army, Transport Division, _____**(Year -17) to** _____**(Year -13)**.
- Jake's Moving Company, _____**(Year -13) to** _____**(Year -10)**.
- Picket Up Delivery Services, _____**(Year -10) to** _____**(Year -0)**.

CONFIDENTIAL FACTS

FOR ATTORNEY FOR DEFENDANT, LANDERS AND PUDS

DEPOSITION OF HOMER PICKET

Date: _____ (**Third Thursday, Month-2**)

Homer Picket

Age: 73 years old, born December 23, _____ **(Year -73).**

Married: Widowed. One daughter, Juliette, age 41.

Education: Nita High School, _____ **(Year -55).**

Employment:

- U.S. Marine Corp. (ret. Master Gunnery Sgt.), _____ **(Year -53) to** _____ **(Year -23).**

- Owner, Picket Up Delivery Services, _____ **(Year -23) to present.**

CONFIDENTIAL FACTS

FOR ATTORNEY FOR DEFENDANT, LANDERS AND PUDS

DEPOSITION OF PERRY REINHART

Date: _____ **(Third Friday, Month -2)**

Perry Reinhart (Co-worker of Mel Landers)

Age:　　26 years old, born August 23, _____**(Year -26)**.

Married:　Married. Two sons.

Education:　Nita High School, _____**(Year -8)**.

Employment:

- Jake's Moving Company, _____ **(Year -8) to** _____**(Year -6)**.
- Picket Up Delivery Services, _____**(Year -6) to present**.

CONFIDENTIAL FACTS

FOR ATTORNEY FOR DEFENDANT, LANDERS AND PUDS

EXPERT MEDICAL REPORT

C.R. Strickland, MD
Nita State University Hospital
Nita City, Nita

Date _____ **(First Monday, Month -6)**

Dr. C.R. Strickland

Age: 49.

Married: Married, four children.

Education: Johns Hopkins University, MD, _____ **(Year -20)**.

Baltimore General Hospital, Internship, _____**(Year -20)** to _____**(Year -18)**.

Nita State University Hospital, Residency,_____**(Year -18)** to _____**(Year -14)**.

Employment:

- Private Practice in Neurosurgery, _____**(Year -13) to present**.
- Teaching Physician and Neurosurgeon, Nita State University Hospital, _____**(Year -10) to present**.

SUPPLEMENTARY REPORT

Re: Patient Number 02845—Helen Darngood

Admitted to Nita State University Hospital Emergency Center at 7:29 p.m., December 23, _____ **(Year -2)**.

I received my medical degree from Johns Hopkins University in _____**(Year -20)**, and after serving a two-year internship at Baltimore General Hospital, I was licensed to practice medicine in _____**(Year -18)**. I served my four-year residency at Nita State University Hospital, after which I established a private practice specializing in the field of neurosurgery here in Nita City, Nita.

I am a board-certified neurosurgeon and have served in multiple medical societies. I am currently on the board of the Nita State University Hospital. Following my residence I have been involved in the practice of medicine for the last fourteen years.

I have studied and analyzed all the medical reports for Helen Darngood. These include the emergency technician and hospital admission reports on December 23, _____**(Year -2)**. I have studied all reports of Ms. Darngood's rehabilitation and medical diagnosis. I have examined tests and have personally examined the patient three times for one-plus hours each time. The most recent time was five days ago.

At 7:30 p.m., on December 23, _____**(Year -2)**, I was called to the Emergency/Trauma Room of Nita State University Hospital. Emergency Medical Services (EMS) were enroute to the Emergency/Trauma Center with a patient directly from the scene of a pedestrian/motor vehicle accident that occurred at Seventh and Smith approximately thirty minutes before.

The EMS technicians provided their initial exam findings upon arrival at the accident as follows:

Pulse:	100 beats per minute
Respirations:	24 breaths per minute
Blood Pressure:	90/50 mm Hg
Head:	Has a large contusion with swelling on the right side of her skull just slightly above her right ear. She has an obvious right black eye, and there is a large bruise forming behind her right ear. She appears to have some blood coming from her right ear, and some clear fluid coming from her nose.
Neck:	Unremarkable
Chest:	Unremarkable except for her heart rate, which is elevated.
Abdomen:	Unremarkable
Pelvis/Back:	Unremarkable
Extremities:	Unremarkable
Neuro:	Patient is unresponsive to voice and eyes are closed. Her right pupil is slightly larger than her left, and the right one does not respond to light. The left one responds to light. She withdraws all of her extremities to painful stimuli, but there is no purposeful movement.

Upon assessing her, the EMS crew astutely placed patient into cervical-spine precautions (rigid collar, long rigid spine board) and transported her to the hospital immediately. Enroute, the patient's airway was controlled with rapid sequence endotrachael intubation, an IV access was established, and an anticonvulsant medication was started.

Enroute to the emergency/trauma center, patient's pulse was 100–114, respirations were 28 and being controlled by a mechanical ventilator, blood pressure was 85–100/50–60. Patient had a single forty-five second, full-motor seizure.

On arrival at the trauma center, patient's vital signs were unchanged. Her airway security was confirmed. Initial evaluation in the emergency department revealed no other injuries. X-rays of her neck, chest, and pelvis showed no fractures, and her abdominal ultrasound was negative for evidence of internal bleeding. External examination revealed no other fractures or contusions. Patient was taken to the computerized tomographic (CT) scanner for further imaging studies.

Patient's CT scan revealed that her only significant injury was a right-sided skull fracture with an underlying epidural hematoma in the temporal lobe region with some axonal shearing injury in her right frontal lobe. Examination showed bruising to patient on left hip and thigh and bruising on right shoulder, upper arm, and right hip. The speed of the impact between the van and patient cannot be determined from the head trauma. Extensive injuries can be caused by seemingly minor impact between patient's head and a fixed or moving object. The strictest medical precautions must be taken when there is any indication of head injury. The epidural hematoma showed evidence of increasing pressure on the right side of her brain. The neurosurgical team, which I lead, made the decision to operate on this immediately to remove the clotted blood that was exerting pressure on the patient's brain. Patient was taken to the operating room and the operation commenced within seventy minutes of her arrival at the trauma center.

During the operation, a right-sided blood clot was removed from the epidural space. A ventriculostomy was performed to monitor her intracranial pressures postoperatively. Her skull fracture was also repaired. The operation was finished after three hours, and patient was taken to the intensive care unit for recovery.

Within twenty-four hours, patient's sedation medication was held, and Helen Darngood began to show signs of waking up. Patient opened her eyes to command and appeared to move all of her extremities to command. On Postoperative Day Two, patient was taken off of the ventilator and was able to breathe on her own. Patient was somewhat confused and disoriented, but seemed to recognize her family. Patient could also follow basic commands. Her intracranial pressures remained within normal limits, and the ventriculostomy was removed on Postoperative Day Three.

On Postoperative Day Four, patient was talking in basic sentences and following all commands. Her condition had stabilized, and she was moved from the intensive care unit to the regular surgical ward of the hospital. Her surgical incision was healing well. Her only problem seemed to be from her right frontal lobe shear injury and intermittent mood swings with agitated behavior and inappropriate verbal tirades. She began to exhibit disinhibited behavior due to her right frontal lobe injury, and the nurses reported that she was undressing inappropriately, demonstrating inappropriate sexual behavior towards others, and using profanity. Her family confirmed this was not normal behavior for her.

While on the regular surgical ward, Helen was visited by the physical and occupational therapy departments, who worked with her in rehabilitative exercises. These teams reported that she was fully capable of completing her own activities of daily living, but seemed to lack motivation. They also confirmed that she was demonstrating a fair amount of agitated, inappropriate behavior and disinhibited speech, consistent with a right frontal lobe injury. On Postoperative Day Eight, patient was transferred to the rehabilitation area of the hospital.

The patient spent a total of eight more days in the rehabilitation area. While there, the patient underwent intensive therapy and was also placed on mood-stabilizing medications in an effort to control her inappropriate behavior and verbal outbursts. There was improvement, and her family was taught how to care for her at home. Her discharge planning included a visit to the physical and occupational therapy clinics every other day, a home nurse visit once per day, and a follow-up visit with her neurosurgeon in one week. Patient was kept on anticonvulsant and mood-stabilizing medication. Patient was happy to be going home and seemed to fully understand her condition. She still had occasional behavioral outbursts and inappropriate speech.

At the present time, Helen is on a single mood-stabilizing medication. She remains on anticonvulsant medication and has been seizure free. Because of the likelihood of seizures, depression, and personality issues, patient will be required to remain on both anticonvulsant medication and mood-stabilizing medication for the foreseeable future. Without anticonvulsant medication, patient and her husband have been advised that she can expect intermittent seizures of varying intensity (petit mal to grand mal). Although the patient has not had a seizure, it was explained to her and her husband that a grand mal seizure can cause unconsciousness, loss of bladder and bowel control, and other injuries such as bruising and possible biting of tongue. The patient and her husband have been told while there is a slight possibility that she will do so, the patient should not experience seizures while taking medication. The combination of both drugs will slow the cognitive function and reaction time of patient. Patient has been advised not to drive a motor vehicle. She no longer visits the physical or occupational therapists and has resumed a somewhat normal life. Patient recently underwent neuropsychological testing, which showed that she has very little memory of the accident or of the six months following it. She tried to go back to work, but was not able to do so, even on a limited basis. She still has occasional emotional outbursts, but these are more rare of late, and with medication she has been able to control her speech and other behaviors much better.

Helen's family has reported to me that the past months have been very hard on all of them. Helen is not the same person.

C. R. Strickland, MD

C. R. Strickland, MD

APPENDICES

APPENDIX A

DIRECTIONS

Representation of Multiple Clients

According to Rule 1.7 of the Model Rules of Professional Conduct: Conflict of Interest: Current Clients, representation of multiple clients in a single matter is permissible. Representation of multiple clients may occur when the clients consent to the representation after consultation with the attorney and an explanation by the attorney of the implications of the common representation as well as the advantages and risks involved. Here, because both Defendant Mel Landers and Defendant Picket Up Delivery Services have consented to be represented by the same attorney and have waived all actual and potential conflicts of interest, Rule 1.7 permits counsel for the defendants to represent both parties. Therefore, defendants' counsel may represent both Mel Landers and Picket Up Delivery Services in this lawsuit.

Burden of Proof

Court or Jury Trial

The Plaintiff shall have the burden of proof by a preponderance of the evidence.

Order of Presentation and Rules of Evidence

Court or Jury Trial

- Helen Darngood is the Plaintiff. Mel Landers and Picket Up Delivery Services are the Defendants.

- The Plaintiff must present evidence first.

- The Plaintiff may not call Defendants' or defense witnesses as witnesses in its case-in-chief.

- Local rules governing the Order of Opening Statement and Final Argument:

  Option 1: The Plaintiff shall present the first opening statement and the concluding final argument. The Defendants shall not have a rebuttal final argument.

  Option 2: The Plaintiff shall present the first opening statement. The Plaintiff shall present the first final argument followed by the Defendant. The Plaintiff shall have a rebuttal final argument.

- The Rules of Evidence, Procedure and Law of the jurisdiction (or the Federal Rules of Evidence) where the complaint is filed shall govern but shall not amend any terms of this agreement.

Suggested Time Schedules

The following schedule indicates how the time may be allocated. The time available for opening statement, witness examination, and final argument may be allocated as the attorneys wish. Objections and arguments will be counted against the attorney that is speaking.

Court Trial—Three Hours

Each side has sixty (60) minutes available and will be responsible for keeping track of its time.

Preliminary Discussion	10 minutes
Plaintiff	60 minutes*
Defendant	60 minutes*
Final Argument	10 minutes

Critique	30 minutes
Breaks	20 minutes

* Opening statement	5 minutes
Direct examination	30 minutes
Cross-examination	15 minutes
Final argument	10 minutes

Jury Trial—Six hours and fifteen minutes

Each side has ninety (90) minutes plus ten (10) minutes for jury selection. The trial may take less time; however, the total time should not exceed six (6) hours and fifteen (15) minutes.

Preliminary Discussion	30 minutes
Judge's Introduction (in jury trial)	10 minutes
Jury Selection (10 minutes per side)	20 minutes
Plaintiff	90 minutes*
Defendant	90 minutes*
Judge's Final Instructions	10 minutes
Jury Deliberation	30 minutes
Critique By Jury	15 minutes
Critique By Judge	30 minutes
Breaks	20 minutes
Lunch	30 minutes

* Opening statement	10 minutes
Direct examination	45 minutes
Cross-examination	20 minutes
Final argument	15 minutes

Expert Witnesses

Only called as witnesses when expert witness examination is part of the exercise. Each expert witness examination adds thirty (30) minutes per side (twenty (20) minutes for direct examination and ten (10) minutes for cross-examination).

When expert witness examinations *are* a part of the exercise, the admissibility and use of expert witness reports are governed by the Rules of Evidence.

When expert witness examinations *are not* a part of this exercise, the reports of the expert witnesses *are* admissible. The expert reports should be marked as exhibits and entered into evidence before opening statements. Both parties may refer to the reports in opening statement and final argument. In a trial the judge *may* provide the report to the jury.

Negotiation and Mediation

The time schedules for negotiation and mediation exercises will be determined by faculty.

Darngood v. Landers and PUDS, Plaintiff

APPENDIX B

NITA APPLICABLE LAW

NITA APPLICABLE LAW

Nita Statutes

169A.20. Driving while impaired.

Subdivision 1. Driving while impaired crime. It is a crime for any person to drive, operate, or be in physical control of any motor vehicle within this state or on any boundary water of this state:

(1) when the person is under the influence of alcohol;

(2) when the person is under the influence of a controlled substance;

(3) when the person is knowingly under the influence of a hazardous substance that affects the nervous system, brain, or muscles of the person so as to substantially impair the person's ability to drive or operate the motor vehicle;

(4) when the person is under the influence of a combination of any two or more of the elements named in clauses (1), (2), and (3);

(5) when the person's alcohol concentration at the time, or as measured within two hours of the time, of driving, operating, or being in physical control of the motor vehicle is 0.08 or more;

(6) when the vehicle is a commercial motor vehicle and the person's alcohol concentration at the time, or as measured within two hours of the time, of driving, operating, or being in physical control of the commercial motor vehicle is 0.04 or more; or

(7) when the person's body contains any amount of a controlled substance listed in schedule I or II other than marijuana or tetrahydrocannabinols.

169A.40. Arrest powers.

Subdivision 1. Probable cause arrest. A peace officer may lawfully arrest a person for violation of section 169A.20 (driving while impaired) without a warrant upon probable cause, without regard to whether the violation was committed in the officer's presence.

169A.41. Preliminary screening test.

Subdivision 1. When authorized. When a peace officer has reason to believe from the manner in which a person is driving, operating, controlling, or acting upon departure from a motor vehicle, or has driven, operated or controlled a motor vehicle, that the driver may be violating or has violated section 169A.20 (driving while impaired), the officer may require the driver to provide a sample of the driver's breath for a preliminary screening test.

Subd. 2. Use of test results. The results of this preliminary screening test may be used for the purpose of deciding whether an arrest should be made and whether to require other tests (chemical tests for intoxication), but must not be used in any court action except the following: in a civil action arising out of the operation or use of the motor vehicle.

169A.51. Chemical tests for intoxication.

Subdivision 1. Implied consent; conditions; election of test.

(1) Any person who drives, operates, or is in physical control of a motor vehicle within this state or on any boundary water of this state consents, subject to the provision of sections 169A.50 to 169A.53 (implied consent law), and section 169A.20 (driving while impaired), to a chemical test of that

person's blood, breath, or urine for the purpose of determining the presence of alcohol, controlled substances, or hazardous substances. The test must be administered at the direction of a peace officer.

(2) The test may be required of a person when an officer has probable cause to believe the person was driving, operating, or in physical control of a motor vehicle in violation of section 169A.20 (driving while impaired), and one of the following conditions exist:

(a) the person has been lawfully placed under arrest for violation of section 169A.20;

(b) the person has been involved in a motor vehicle accident or collision resulting in property damage, personal injury, or death.

Subd. 2. Implied consent advisory. At the time a test is requested, the person must be informed:

(1) that state law requires the person to take a test;

(a) to determine if the person is under the influence of alcohol, controlled substances, or hazardous substances;

(2) that refusal to take a test is a crime;

(3) that the person has the right to consult with an attorney, but this right is limited to the extent that it cannot unreasonably delay administration of the test.

Subd. 3. Type of test. The peace officer who requires a test pursuant to this section may direct whether the test is of blood, breath, or urine. Action may be taken against a person who refuses to take a blood test only if an alternative test was offered, and action may be taken against a person who refuses to take a urine test only if an alternative test was offered.

169.06. Signs, signals, markings.

Subdivision 1. Obedience to traffic-control signal or flagger; presumptions. The driver of any vehicle shall obey the instructions of any official traffic-control device applicable thereto placed in accordance with the provisions of this chapter.

Subd. 2. Traffic-control signal. Whenever traffic is controlled by traffic-control signals exhibiting different colored lights, or colored lighted arrows, successively one at a time or in combination, only the colors Green, Red, and Yellow shall be used, except for special pedestrian signals carrying a word or legend. The traffic-control signal lights or colored lighted arrows indicate and apply to drivers of vehicles and pedestrians as follows:

(1) Green indication:

(a) Vehicular traffic facing a circular green signal may proceed straight through or turn right or left unless a sign at such place prohibits either turn. But vehicular traffic, including vehicles turning right or left, shall yield the right-of-way to other vehicles and to pedestrians lawfully within the intersection or adjacent crosswalk at the time this signal is exhibited.

(b) Vehicular traffic facing a green arrow signal, shown alone or in combination with another indication, may cautiously enter the intersection only to make the movement indicated by the arrow, or other movement as permitted by other indications shown at the same time. Such vehicular traffic shall yield the right-of-way to pedestrians lawfully within an adjacent crosswalk and to other traffic lawfully using the intersection.

(c) Unless otherwise directed by a pedestrian-control signal, pedestrians facing any green signal, except when the sole green signal is a turn arrow, may proceed across the roadway within any marked or unmarked crosswalk. Every driver of a vehicle shall yield the right-of-way

Darngood v. Landers and PUDS, Plaintiff

to such pedestrian, except that the pedestrian shall yield the right-of-way to vehicles lawfully within the intersection at the time that the green signal indication is first shown.

(2) Steady yellow indication:

    (a) Vehicular traffic facing a circular yellow signal is thereby warned that the related green movement is being terminated or that a red indication will be exhibited immediately thereafter. A vehicle may enter an intersection upon a yellow signal and may proceed through the intersection with caution.

(3) Steady red indication:

    (a) Upon a red indication, vehicular traffic must not enter the intersection.

    (b) Vehicular traffic facing a circular red signal alone must stop at a clearly marked stop line but, if none, before entering the crosswalk on the near side of the intersection or, if none, then before entering the intersection and shall remain standing until a green indication is shown.

    (c) At a pedestrian-control signal, pedestrians facing a steady red signal alone shall not enter the roadway.

169.14. Speed limits.

Subdivision 1. Duty to drive with due care. No person shall drive a vehicle on a roadway at a speed greater than is reasonable and prudent under the conditions. Every driver is responsible for becoming and remaining aware of the actual and potential hazards then existing on the roadway and must use due care in operating a vehicle. In every event speed shall be so restricted as may be necessary to avoid colliding with any person, vehicle, or other conveyance on or entering the roadway in compliance with legal requirements and the duty of all persons to use due care.

Subd. 2. Speed limits. Where no special hazard exists the following speeds shall be lawful, but any speeds in excess of such limits shall be prima facie evidence that the speed is not reasonable or prudent and that it is unlawful; except that the speed limit within any municipality shall be a maximum limit and any speed in excess thereof shall be unlawful: 30 miles per hour in an urban district or on a town road in a rural residential district.

Subd. 3. Reduced speed required. The driver of any vehicle shall, consistent with the requirements, drive at an appropriate reduced speed when approaching and crossing an intersection and when special hazards exist with respect to pedestrians or other traffic or by reason of weather or roadway conditions.

169.21. Pedestrian. Obey traffic-control signals.

Pedestrians shall be subject to traffic-control signals at intersections as heretofore declared in this chapter and shall keep a reasonable lookout for their own safety, but at all other places pedestrians shall be accorded the privileges and shall be subject to the restrictions stated in this section.

169.96. Interpretation and effect.

(1) This chapter shall be interpreted and construed as to effectuate its general purpose to make uniform the law of those states which enact it.

(2) In all civil actions, a violation of any of the provisions of this chapter, by either or any of the parties to such action or actions shall not be negligence per se but shall be prima facie evidence of negligence only.

169.101. Burden of proof.

The provisions of this chapter shall not be construed to relieve the plaintiff in any civil action from the burden of proving negligence on the part of the defendant as the proximate cause of an accident.

541.05. Various cases, six years.

Subdivision 1. Six-year limitation. Except where the Uniform Commercial Code otherwise prescribes, the following actions shall be commenced within six years:

(1) Upon a liability created by statute;

(2) For any other injury to the person or rights of another, not arising on contract, and not hereinafter enumerated.

604.01. Comparative fault; effect.

Subdivision 1. Scope of application. Contributory fault does not bar recovery in an action by any person or the person's legal representative to recover damages for fault resulting in death, in injury to person or property, or in economic loss, if the contributory fault was not greater than the fault of the person against whom recovery is sought, but any damages allowed must be diminished in proportion to the amount of fault attributable to the person recovering. The court may, and when requested by any party shall, direct the jury to find separate special verdicts determining the amount of damages and the percentage of fault attributable to each party, and the court shall then reduce the amount of damages in proportion to the amount of fault attributable to the person recovering.

Subd. 2. Fault. "Fault" includes acts or omissions that are in any measure negligent or reckless toward the person or property of the actor or others, or that subject a person to strict tort liability. The term also includes breach of warranty, unreasonable assumption of risk not constituting an express consent or primary assumption of risk, misuse of a product and unreasonable failure to avoid an injury or to mitigate damages, and the defense of complicity. Legal requirements of causal relation apply both to fault as the basis for liability and to contributory fault. The doctrine of last clear chance is abolished.

Evidence of unreasonable failure to avoid aggravating an injury or to mitigate damages may be considered only in determining the damages to which the claimant is entitled. It may not be considered in determining the cause of an accident.

APPENDIX C

MANUAL FOR THE WHEELED VEHICLE DRIVER
DEPARTMENTS OF ARMY AND AIR FORCE

Appendix C—Manual for the Wheeled Vehicle Driver
Departments of Army and Air Force
Page 1 of 4

MANUAL FOR THE WHEELED VEHICLE DRIVER

Headquarters

Department of the Army

Department of the Air Force

Field Manual

____(Year -20)

CHAPTER 2

Traffic Signals

No traffic signal is more important than the traffic light (Fig. 2-2). Few drivers actually run through red lights. Their common sense usually keeps them from that. They speed up as they approach a green light to make sure they get through before it turns red; or when stopped at a red light, they watch the green light showing in the opposite direction and start to move into the intersection as soon as the yellow appears. This practice often results in an accident.

Figure 2. Traffic Signals

RED

Stop—come to a complete stop before reaching the intersection, stop line, or crosswalk, and remain stopped as long as the light is red.

YELLOW

Caution—an amber or yellow light is a warning that the light is about to change. If the driver has not entered the intersection, the driver should come to a safe stop. If the driver is already in the intersection, the driver should continue moving and clear it safely. Speeding up to "beat the light" is illegal and could cause an accident.

GREEN

Go—the driver may go through an intersection in the direction indicated by the signal if the roadway is clear.

Traffic Signs

The United States is moving toward an international system of traffic signs that emphasizes pictures and symbols rather than written messages. Symbolic signs are not entirely new. The familiar curve and crossroad symbols have been used for many years. Symbols have several advantages over word messages. They provide almost instant communication to the driver since they can be understood at a glance without having to be read. Also, they overcome language barriers.

Appendix C—Manual for the Wheeled Vehicle Driver
Departments of Army and Air Force
Page 2 of 4

CHAPTER 3

Speed Control

Speed not only makes accidents more likely, but also makes death in accidents more likely. There are several statutes in each state in the United States dealing with speed. The most important and common sense rule is: NO PERSON SHALL DRIVE A VEHICLE ON A HIGHWAY AT A SPEED GREATER THAN IS REASONABLE AND PRUDENT UNDER THE EXISTING CONDITIONS. However, conditions are constantly changing, and it may be necessary to drive slower than the posted speed limit. Speed affects the ability to turn, pass, slow down, and stop.

Stopping

The following factors affect the driver's ability to bring the vehicle to a stop:

- Type and condition of road surface, such as concrete, asphalt, or gravel.

- Foreign material on the road, such as ice, snow, leaves, or mud.

- Road configuration, such as uphill or downhill, straight, curve, high crown, or dip.

- Tire condition, such as type and condition of tread and tire inflation.

- Brakes, such as type and state of repair and adjustment.

For any speed, the distance required to stop a vehicle in an emergency depends on three things—driver perception time, driver reaction time, and vehicle stopped time. During driver perception time and driver reaction time, the vehicle slows down very little because the brakes have not yet been applied.

Perception Distance

Perception distance is that distance traveled between the time a dangerous situation is first seen by the driver and the time the driver actually recognizes it as being dangerous. This time varies widely in different situations. The distance traveled will vary with the speed of the vehicle and the individual mental response of the driver.

Reaction Distance

Reaction distance is that distance traveled by a vehicle during which the driver determines the preventive action to be taken and actually sets the vehicle controls in motion. In stopping, it would include the time required to move the foot from the accelerator to the brake pedal. Some emergencies require complex reactions involving decisions to turn, increase speed, or stop, and consequently require increased time for the driver to decide how to react.

Braking Distance

Ability to slow down depends on how hard and steadily the operator presses the brake, how efficient the brakes are compared to the weight of the vehicle and its load, and how slippery the road surface is. Most vehicles can be stopped on a dry road surface within the distance required by state laws, but snow, ice, rain, and gravel reduce the vehicle's stopping ability and increase the distance necessary to bring the vehicle to a complete stop.

Appendix C—Manual for the Wheeled Vehicle Driver
Departments of Army and Air Force
Page 3 of 4

Avoiding Collisions

Many times a driver can avoid a collision merely by slowing down. Even after it is too late to stop or slow down, a driver may often avoid a collision by swerving to one side. It is normally safer to swerve to the right than to the left. It is better to run off the road to the right than to collide head on. However, a speeding vehicle cannot be turned sharply without the risk of turning over. The faster a vehicle is going the more distance it takes to turn safely from a straight path.

CHAPTER 6

Intersections

The most dangerous place on a street or highway is an intersection. An elementary law of physics says that two bales cannot occupy the same space at the same time. Hundreds of thousands of drivers and pedestrians have demonstrated the truth of this law by losing their lives at intersections. An intersection is any place where two more roads join or cross each other. Drivers are required to slow down when approaching all intersections—whether or not the driver has the right-of-way. The following rules of the road are normal; however, state and local laws take precedence. The main question faced by drivers at an intersection is: "Who has the right-of-way?"

Intersections with Traffic Controls

Traffic Lights

Traffic lights greatly simplify right-of-way problems since the traffic on one road is stopped while the traffic on the other is permitted to proceed. For vehicles coming from opposite directions on the road that has the green light, the right-of-way rules are the same as those that would apply in absence of traffic signals.

CHAPTER 7

Pedestrians, Bicyclists, and Animals

Pedestrians, bicyclists, and animals pose special problems for drivers. It is often difficult to see pedestrians, bicyclists, and animals on the road. Drivers must be alert to avoid collisions with them.

Pedestrians

Pedestrians are a poor match for the automobile. In the United States, about 10,000 of them are killed in traffic accidents each year. When pedestrians are involved in collisions, speeds of no greater than 15 or 20 mph often prove fatal.

It is true that pedestrians often violate laws passed for their protection. They may walk along highways with their backs to oncoming traffic. They often ignore crosswalks and cross in the middle of a block. Children dart out into the street without looking for traffic. Nevertheless, after one has killed a child, it is not much comfort to know that the child was at least partly to blame. Pedestrians will be safe on streets and highways only when drivers are willing to be their brothers' keeper.

A driver should let the pedestrian know the driver's intentions. Whenever a pedestrian may be affected by a driver turning, stopping, or starting, the law requires the driver blow the horn regardless of

Appendix C—Manual for the Wheeled Vehicle Driver
Departments of Army and Air Force
Page 4 of 4

who has the right-of-way. Be careful how the horn is blown. A long, loud blast can frighten and confuse a pedestrian, increasing instead of minimizing the danger. Use the horn as a warning signal, not as a command to get out of the way. Whenever a driver blows the horn to warn a pedestrian, the driver's foot should be off the accelerator and ready to depress the brake pedal.

Anticipate the pedestrian's intentions. If a driver sees a person in the street, the driver should slow down and get ready to stop. The pedestrian may be able to take care, but do not depend on it. The pedestrian may get confused and walk right in front of the driver.

At intersections controlled by ordinary traffic lights, pedestrians obey the same signals as drivers. When crossing on green light, they have the right-of-way. If a light changes to yellow or red while a pedestrian is still in the street, drivers must allow the pedestrian to complete crossing safely.

At some intersections, special lights instruct pedestrians either to walk or to wait. Where these lights are in operation, pedestrians must obey them instead of the regular traffic lights. Pedestrians crossing on a special pedestrian signal have the right-of-way just as they do when crossing on a green light.

If a driver is going through an intersection on a green light and a pedestrian starts to cross in front of the driver against a red light, warn the pedestrian by sounding the horn. If the pedestrian does not stop, the driver must stop. If a life is saved, losing the right-of-way will be worthwhile. The safe driver yields the right-of-way to a pedestrian when the pedestrian is entitled to it and even when the pedestrian is not.

CHAPTER 11

Hazards and Safety Measures

Smoking, Eating, and Drinking

The use of tobacco and alcohol reduces a driver's ability to see. Eating, smoking, and drinking impair senses. Never eat or smoke when operating a vehicle, and do not drink alcoholic beverages eight hours before or when driving.

Darngood v. Landers and PUDS, Plaintiff

APPENDIX D
JOINT STATEMENT OF CASE

STATE OF NITA

COUNTY OF DARROW

DISTRICT COURT

SECOND JUDICIAL DISTRICT

HELEN DARNGOOD

        Plaintiff

v.

MEL LANDERS, AN INDIVIDUAL,

AND PICKET UP DELIVERY SERVICES,

A NITA CORPORATION

        Defendants.

JOINT STATEMENT OF CASE

Court File No. 3543
Case type: Personal Injury

---

1. All parties have been served with process. The case is at issue, and the parties have joined in the filing of this Joint Statement of the Case.

2. Estimated trial time: __1__ day.

3. Jury is requested by the ☒ plaintiff ☒ defendants. (If this is a change from a court to a jury request, then a $75 fee must be paid when filing this document.)

4. Concise statement of the case including facts plaintiff(s) intend to prove and legal basis for claims:

    On December 23, _____ **(Year -2)**, Picket Up Delivery Services held a company holiday party for all of its employees. The party lasted from 3:00 to 7:00 p.m. Mel Landers attended this company holiday party at 3:30 p.m. Mel Landers left the party early to make the last delivery of the day so Landers could get home to Landers's son. Driving home, Mel Landers drove the delivery van west on Smith Street. As Landers proceeded through the intersection of Smith Street and Seventh Street, Landers's van struck Ms. Darngood, who was crossing the street in a marked crosswalk. Mel Landers was given a field sobriety and intoxilyzer test. The attending officer did not issue a citation to Mel Landers. Ms. Darngood was transported to the hospital with a head injury.

    Ms. Darngood intends to prove that Mel Landers negligently drove and struck Ms. Darngood on December 23, _____ **(Year -2)**, resulting in severe damage to Ms. Darngood. Specifically, Ms. Darngood intends to prove that Mel Landers drove negligently at the intersection of Smith Avenue and Seventh Street and, thereby, struck Ms. Darngood while she was in a marked crosswalk with a green light giving her the right of way.

    The parties agree that at the time of the accident Mel Landers acted within the scope of employment while working as an employee of Picket Up Delivery Services.

5. Concise statement of the case including facts defendants intend to prove and legal basis for claims:

Defendants Mel Landers and Picket Up Delivery Services intend to prove that Ms. Darngood negligently crossed the street on December 23,_____ **(Year -2)**. Specifically, Defendants intend to prove that Ms. Darngood entered into the intersection of Smith Avenue and Seventh Street without taking the proper care. In doing so, Mel Landers intends to prove that Ms. Darngood's negligence was the cause of the accident. Thus, neither Mel Landers nor Picket Up Delivery Services were liable.

- List the names and addresses of witnesses known to either party that either party may call. Indicate the party who expects to call the witness and whether the party intends to qualify that witness as an expert.

Party	Name/Address of Witness	Please Indicate if Expert Witness
Plaintiff	Cooper Earle, 613 MontCalm Blvd., Nita City, Nita	Lay Witness
Plaintiff	Helen Darngood, 1330 Lakeview Lane, Nita City, Nita	Lay Witness
Plaintiff	George Carpenter, 1330 Lakeview Lane, Nita City, Nita	Lay Witness
Plaintiff	Margaret Hanson, 515 Porter Way, Nita City, Nita	Lay Witness
Plaintiff	Dr. C.R. Strickland Nita State University Hospital, Nita City, Nita	Expert Witness
Defendant	Mel Landers, 5151 Sherwood Forest Blvd., Middleboro, Nita	Lay Witness
Defendant	Homer Picket 1965 Industrial Blvd., Nita City, Nita	Lay Witness
Defendant	Perry Reinhart, 1645 Laurel Ave., Apt. 1, Middleboro, Nita	Lay Witness

6. In claims involving personal injury, attach a statement by each claimant, whether by complaint or counterclaim, setting forth a detailed description of claimed injuries and an itemized list of special damages as required by the rule. Indicate whether parties will exchange medical reports.

Ms. Darngood details and itemizes the following damages.

- **Past Pain and Suffering:** Ms. Darngood suffered a right skull fracture as well as additional injuries as a result of being struck by the van Mel Landers was driving. Ms. Darngood's injuries resulted in seizures and the need for mood stabilizing and anticonvulsant medication in addition to extensive physical therapy.

- **Future Pain and Suffering:** Ms. Darngood continues to suffer from the injuries she sustained in the accident, and will continue to do so in the future.

- **Lost Income:** Ms. Darngood has lost and will continue to lose income because she is no longer able to maintain her CEO position at Darngood Electronics because of the accident.

- **Medical Expenses:** Medical expenses are *not* an issue in this exercise.

The parties have exchanged medical reports.

7. Additionally, the parties agree as to the preliminary and final jury instructions.

8. The following are facts and issues that remain disputed among the Defendants and Plaintiff.

The parties dispute whether Ms. Darngood or Mel Landers had the right-of-way. The parties dispute who is responsible for the accident. The parties dispute whether Mel Landers and Picket Up Delivery Services or Helen Darngood were negligent. The parties dispute the extent of Ms. Darngood's damages.

The undersigned counsel have met and conferred this _____ **(Monday, Week - 6)** and certify the foregoing is true and correct.

R.W. Fingal

R.W. Fingal

ATTORNEY FOR PLAINTIFF

Scott Phillips

Scott Phillips

ATTORNEY FOR THE DEFENDANTS

APPENDIX E
MEMORANDUM TO SENIOR PARTNER
PRELIMINARY LEGAL AND STRATEGIC ANALYSIS
PLAINTIFF

MEMORANDUM

Client: **Helen Darngood**

To: **Senior Partner**

From: **Associate**

Re: **Preliminary Darngood Case Analysis**

BACKGROUND

Facts

We represent Helen Darngood (Darngood) against Mel Landers (Landers) and Picket Up Delivery Services (PUDS). Landers is an employee of PUDS and drives a PUDS van as part of Landers's employment. Mel Landers and Picket Up Delivery Services admit that Mel Landers was acting in the scope of employment at Picket Up Delivery Services at the time of the accident. On December 23, _____ **(Year -2)**, Landers was driving a PUDS van for the purpose of making a delivery. Landers's van hit Darngood as Darngood was in the crosswalk at the intersection of Seventh Street and Smith Avenue. Traffic lights controlled the intersection. The parties dispute what color the lights were at the time of the accident. Before the accident, Darngood was President and CEO of Darngood Electronics. Her annual salary was $200,000. Darngood resigned her position following the accident.

Procedural History

We have filed a suit on Darngood's behalf. The statute of limitations has not entered into play. In Nita, a personal injury action based on negligence must be brought within six years. Nita Stat. § 541.05(5); *D.M.S. v. Hair*, 745 Nita 2d 637 **(Year -2)**. The accident occurred less than six years ago.

Theory

Our theory of the case is that Landers, in a hurry to get home, was distracted and potentially intoxicated and negligently drove too fast through the intersection traveling west on Smith Avenue. In addition, Landers was acting within the scope and course of Landers's employment with PUDS at the time of the accident. Therefore PUDS is liable under the doctrine of respondeat superior if we prove that

Landers was liable. *Weiss v. Larson*, 633 Nita 2d 355 **(Year -5)**. At the same time, Darngood proceeded to cross Seventh Street in the crosswalk heading south with a green light. Darngood was not negligent when stepping off the curb as she was immediately struck by Landers. Landers denies negligence. PUDS denies Landers's actions were negligent.

ISSUES

1. Whether Landers and Picket Up Delivery Services were negligent on December 23, ____ **(Year -2)** when Landers's van struck Helen Darngood?

2. Whether Darngood was contributorily at fault for the accident?

3. Is Picket Up Delivery Services liable under the concept of vicarious liability?

4. What damages are available to Darngood?

ANALYSIS

1. Landers's Negligence

Darngood has brought a negligence cause of action against Landers and Picket Up Delivery Services. Generally, negligence is the failure to use reasonable care under the circumstances. *Metropolitan Employees Ret. Fund v. Anson-Williams Co.,* 619 Nita 2d 568 **(Year -12)**. The elements of a typical negligence action are: 1) the existence of a duty; 2) breach of that duty; 3) breach of the duty was the actual and proximate cause of the injury; and 4) damage to person or property. Nita law requires drivers to stop at red lights. Nita Stat. § 169.06 subds. 4, 5(a)(3)(i). A violation is prima facie evidence of negligence. *Id.* § 169.96(b). To rebut this evidence, the violator must 1) establish a reasonable excuse, or 2) justify an assumption that the violation was not negligent and would not endanger anyone protected by the statute. *Hamry v. Zebo*, 532 Nita 2d 281 **(Year -18)**. Landers will have a difficult time rebutting the prima facie proof. Thus, if Darngood can prove Landers was distracted, inattentive, did not keep a proper lookout and was driving too fast, she will likely be able to establish Landers was negligent.

Whereas Landers says the light turned yellow just as the van entered the intersection, this is not clear. The law allows Landers to enter the intersection on a yellow light. The driver can proceed through the intersection with care. Even if Landers is correct about the color of the light, there is a question of whether Landers acted with care when Landers proceeded through the intersection. There is no dispute that the light turned green for Darngood. Taking Landers's version of the facts, the van's speed was 8.18

miles per hour. This is still too fast for the circumstances. Furthermore, if the light turned yellow at some point before the van entered the intersection, the speed increased and Landers is more negligent.

The testimony of Cooper Earle is Darngood's best supporting evidence that Landers was driving too fast and that Darngood had a green light when she entered the crosswalk. Earle will testify seeing Landers speed up before entering the intersection and, in doing so, entered the intersection on a red light. Further, Earle will testify seeing a woman in the crosswalk with a green light and walk signal. Notably, Earle is the only available nonparty eyewitness to the accident.

Other evidence supports Darngood's argument that Landers was negligent. For instance, Landers had a .059 blood-alcohol test one and a half hours after the accident. In addition, Landers had one more delivery to make that evening, and Landers was anxious to make it home to see Landers's son. Also, Landers was required to make the delivery so not to violate PUDS' delivery guarantee. Finally, Landers has a strong motivation to deny driving too fast or being negligent because Landers has two traffic violations at work. If Landers receives a third, Landers will be terminated and will have no way to support the family. However, these two traffic violations may not be admissible per the controlling rules of evidence.

The most damaging evidence against Darngood is that she remembers only that she was the first person to step into the street and was not aware of the van until just before it hit her. As a result, our case against Landers rests on the supporting testimony of Earle. There are a few concerns about the credibility of Earle's testimony. First, Earle may come across as biased because Earle has a fifteen-year casual friendship with Darngood. Second, Earle was almost one full block away when the accident occurred. Third, it was the holiday season and many nearby stores were decorated with colored lights—including the colors red and green—that could have interfered with Earle's perception of the color of the semaphore.

2. Darngood's Contributory Negligence

Landers will likely raise the affirmative defense of contributory fault. Contributory fault is not a per se bar against recovery if the person seeking recovery is not at greater fault than the person being sued. Nita Stat. § 604.01 Subd. 1. Recovery will, however, be reduced "in proportion to the amount of fault attributable to the person recovering." *Id.* A party is at "fault" if the party acted negligently. *Id.* at Subd. 1a. The Darngood case raises two concerns about contributory negligence.

First, a pedestrian has a duty to obey traffic signals in crosswalks. *Id.* at § 169.21 Subd. 1. A violation of this duty is prima facie evidence that the violator was negligent, subject to the same rebuttal standard noted in section 1. *Id.* at § 169.96. According to Landers, Darngood stepped out as Landers entered the intersection on a yellow light. If this is true, Darngood did not obey the traffic signal because she would have had a red light. To corroborate Landers's testimony, the defense will likely attempt to introduce evidence that Darngood had a propensity to be the first one off the curb, implying that Darngood left early. Whether this is admissible or not should be determined in a motion in limine. The dispute will be whether it qualifies as habit and is therefore admissible; or, whether it is character evidence and is kept out. *Compare* Fed. R. Evid. 404(a) *with* 406.

Second, even if Darngood obeyed the traffic light and had the right-of-way, she still had a duty to exercise ordinary care for her own safety. *Thom v. Mullett*, 188 Nita 2d 98 **(Year -48)**. Landers will argue that Darngood was at fault for the accident because she did not look across the street before attempting to cross. Landers will support this assertion with the fact that Darngood was the first person to step into the street. We will have to show that Darngood had the right to rely on the light. Assuming Darngood contributed to the accident to some degree, we will have to somehow reduce this contributory negligence. The cross-examination of Landers will be important to demonstrate that Darngood's behavior was reasonable and typical for an ordinary pedestrian under the same circumstances. Our jury selection questions should be designed to set this up.

3. Liability of PUDS—(Respondeat Superior)

If Landers's conduct constitutes negligence, then PUDS is also liable for that negligence. Under the theory of respondeat superior, employers are liable for the torts of their employees when such employees commit a tort during the scope and course of their employment. *Fahrendorff v. North Homes, Inc.*, 632 Nita 2d 405 **(Year -6)**, *Weiss v. Larson*, 633 Nita 2d 355 **(Year -5)**. Where the tortious actions of the employee are foreseeable, it is also likely the employee was acting within the scope of employment. *Hagen v. Burmeister & Assoc., Inc.*, 633 Nita 2d 497 **(Year -5)**. It is likely PUDS will be held liable for Landers's negligence.

It is undisputed that Landers was making a PUDS delivery and driving a PUDS delivery van at the time of the accident. It is likely Landers was acting within the scope of Landers's employment at the time of the accident because it was Landers's job to make deliveries to PUDS' customers using the PUDS van. Moreover, the driving was within the scope of Landers's employment because Landers was only driving the PUDS van to make a PUDS delivery. All parties agree that Mel Landers was acting in the scope of employment for PUDS when making a delivery at the time of the accident and therefore through stipulation the doctrine of respondeat superior applies. We must make it clear to the fact finder that PUDS and Landers as Defendants are equally responsible. We should be able to obtain more significant compensation for our client than if Landers alone was the Defendant.

4. Compensatory Damages

Darngood bears the burden of proving past and future damages with reasonable certainty by a preponderance of the evidence. *Rowen v. May*, 802 Nita 2d 33 **(Year -1)** (past damages); *Peterson v. Egg*, 395 Nita 2d 568 **(Year -26)** (future damages). Most notably, the plaintiff will prove Darngood's entire life has changed. She no longer is a high-ranking executive, she is often depressed, and she endured significant difficulties rehabilitating from her injuries. We must demonstrate that she will take medication all her life to prevent seizures. The medication makes it impossible for her to work at a level that allows her to keep an executive position. She will experience slower cognitive function and reaction time. While she resigned voluntarily, she really had no other option. Nonetheless, the future duration of these injuries may be speculative because not only has she chosen to refrain from working a replacement job, she spends more time with her family now.

Her doctor says it is possible but unlikely she will experience seizures while taking medication. Ms. Darngood lives in constant fear of seizures. We must demonstrate what happens during a seizure, that a seizure is very traumatic, and that Ms. Darngood's fear is reasonable.

We do not want to appear to overreach. While Ms. Darngood will not be able to work at the same level she once did, she still has significant financial resources and the company is a family company. While there is a loss of income, medical costs, and pain and suffering, the long-term damage is in her substantially reduced quality of life. We must provide a reasonable method to calculate this loss. For example, we could argue in final argument that a damage value of $25/hour for sixteen hours per day (awake time) over thirty years is more than four million dollars. We will have to determine if our jurisdiction permits us to use this kind of calculation in final argument. By suing both Landers and Picket Up Delivery Services, we have the potential to recover more than if we sue Landers alone. The stipulation that Landers was acting in the scope of employment while working for Picket Up Delivery Services at the time of the accident increases the opportunity to recover more substantial compensation because it will be difficult for the Defendants to personalize the company.

CONCLUSION

Assuming the jury finds Landers negligent, it may still assign some percent of fault to Darngood for failing to look before crossing the street. If the jury finds Landers negligent, the jury will also likely find PUDS vicariously liable. As for damages, Darngood has suffered significant damages as a result of the accident and is entitled to be compensated. It will be a challenge to prove substantial future damages. We will have to demonstrate how dramatic the change in her life is. We will want to show she is only half the person she once was.

APPENDIX F

MEMORANDUM TO SENIOR PARTNER
PRELIMINARY LEGAL AND STRATEGIC ANALYSIS
DEFENDANTS

MEMORANDUM

Client: **Defendant Mel Landers and Defendant Picket Up Delivery Services**

To: **Senior Partner**

From: **Associate**

Re: **Preliminary Landers Case Memorandum**

INTRODUCTION

The objective of this memo is to identify and to analyze the relevant legal issues as well as to provide case strategy recommendations so that counsel is adequately prepared for trial.

This suit arises out of a pedestrian/vehicle accident that occurred on December 23, _____ **(Year -2)**. The plaintiff alleges our clients, Mel Landers (Landers) and Picket Up Delivery Services (PUDS) (Landers's employer), are liable for her injuries. Specifically, the plaintiff alleges Landers negligently drove the PUDS vehicle into the crosswalk, striking the plaintiff and causing her injuries. Landers denies any negligence. Landers claims the van slowly entered the intersection on a yellow light and Landers proceeded through the intersection carefully. Our clients claim the plaintiff was 100 percent contributorily negligent because she did not keep a careful lookout and stepped in front of the van. Mel Landers and Picket Up Delivery Services agree that Mel Landers was acting within the scope of employment while working for Picket Up Delivery Services at the time of the accident. Both parties agree that we can represent both of them and that they waive any actual or potential conflict of interest.

FACTS

Landers has been a van driver for PUDS for ten years. Landers is thirty-five years old and is a single parent. Landers's spouse died from cancer three years ago. Prior to the accident Landers committed two traffic violations. PUDS has a traffic violation policy that states that a third traffic violation or a violation resulting in personal injury is cause for termination. Thus, Landers faces potential termination by PUDS. The day of the accident, PUDS hosted a holiday party where they served alcohol and food. Our client arrived at the party around 3:30 p.m. and left prior to 7:00 p.m. Landers says two or three beers were consumed and that the last drink was at about 6:30. Another PUDS employee says Landers had a couple of beers, ate a lot of food, and was not intoxicated. The police report says that Landers passed the field sobriety test and that Landers's speech wasn't slurred, but that Landers's eyes were a bit red. The police performed an intoxilyzer test, which reported a .059 BAC value. No citations were issued due to conflicting testimony and the lack of witnesses.

The accident occurred around 7:00 p.m. at the intersection of Seventh Street, a busy arterial street running north/south, and Smith Avenue. The north/south semaphores can only be seen by persons looking either north or south. The same is true for the east/west semaphores. The lights are timed and do not change at the same time. Outside it was dark, the street lights were on, and every fifty feet above the streets there were hanging evergreen garlands. The street scene was filled with extraordinary visual clutter from things such as holiday building lights, window and street displays, and holiday shoppers.

The client's version of the accident is that Landers was driving west on Smith, at under 20 mph, and prior to entering the intersection Landers's light was green; yet, as Landers entered the intersection, the light turned yellow. Landers did not speed up to go through; however, a woman suddenly stepped off the curb in front of the van, and Landers could not stop in time to avoid hitting her. Cooper Earle, the only witness at the scene, said that he (Earle) was approximately sixty feet from the intersection when he saw a PUDS truck enter the intersection from the east. Earle was facing north, and the van came from Earle's right. Earle also stated the light was green for the north/south traffic and that the van speeded up to over 20 mph when it entered the intersection. As the van entered the intersection, a lone woman stepped into the crosswalk and was hit by the van. Earle related tiredness that evening and having known the plaintiff for over fifteen years. The law allows a driver to enter an intersection on yellow, but the driver must then proceed with care. If Landers's version is true and Darngood started to cross on the green, Landers's van traveled 66 feet in 5.5 seconds, or 8.2 miles per hour. We have to show this is reasonable. If the light changed to yellow at some point before Landers entered the intersection the speed will be faster.

DISCUSSION

The central issue in this case is whether our client was negligent. For the plaintiff to establish a prima facie case for negligence, she will need to prove the following elements by a preponderance of the evidence: 1) the existence of a duty on the part of Mel Landers to conform to a specific standard of conduct for the protection of the plaintiff against an unreasonable risk of injury; 2) the breach of that duty by Mel Landers; 3) the breach of duty by Mel Landers was the actual and proximate cause of the plaintiff's injury; and, 4) the presence of damage to plaintiff's person.

The duty of reasonable care includes: 1) the duty of every person using the roadway as a driver or a pedestrian to maintain a reasonable lookout, and 2) the duty of a driver to keep driver's vehicle under control. Nita Stat. § 169.14 and § 169.21. Also, the duty of reasonable care may be set by statute in certain circumstances under the negligence per se doctrine. Potential sources of statutory negligence for

Landers are Nita Stat. § 169.06, Subd. 5(a)(1) and Nita Stat. § 169A.20. Nita Stat. § 169.06 says a driver's failure to yield to a pedestrian who is lawfully in a crosswalk is prima facie evidence of negligence. However, a pedestrian must exercise ordinary care for his own safety even though he is on the crosswalk and has the right-of-way. *Thom v. Mullett*, 188 Nita 2d 98 **(Year -48)**. Nita Stat. § 169A.20 makes it a crime for a person to operate a vehicle while under the influence of alcohol. The question is whether Landers was under the influence and whether we can suppress this evidence. Landers passed all sobriety tests, but alcohol does have an effect on a person. We will need to show that an effect of alcohol did not contribute to the accident. The defendants and the plaintiff owed each other reciprocal duties of care, and a statute may supply this duty of care.

Finding that Landers and PUDS owed the plaintiff a duty of care, did Landers depart from this requisite standard of care? The answer depends on the jury's assessment of witness credibility at trial. If the jury believes that alcohol did not play a role in the accident, then liability may not attach. Another benefit is that the officer maintained the liability facts were inconclusive due to conflicting testimony and witness unavailability. However, if the jury believes the witness's version of the accident or thinks alcohol played a role, then Landers and PUDS breached their duty of care since Landers drove through a yellow light that required more care, may have driven too fast, and/or was influenced by alcohol. The resolution depends on witness credibility and the jury's perceived role of alcohol.

The next issue is whether Landers's conduct was the actual and proximate cause of the plaintiff's injury. Landers's conduct will be the actual cause of the plaintiff's harm if Landers's conduct was a substantial factor in materially contributing to the plaintiff's injury, and it will not be the proximate cause of the plaintiff's harm if, looking back from the harm to the conduct, it appears to the court "highly extraordinary" that the conduct should have brought about the harm. The most probable actual causes of this accident are: 1) Landers's alcohol use; 2) Landers's failure to control the vehicle; 3) Landers's or the plaintiff's failure to maintain lookout; 4) Landers's or the plaintiff's failure to properly yield; 5) ambient visual clutter; and 6) yellow light issues. It is foreseeable that any of these causes would bring about the harm that occurred. Particularly foreseeable is the probability for harm resulting from the use of alcohol prior to driving. Given the facts, it is hard to draw a conclusion on causation; however, it will be problematic for us to overcome Landers's alcohol use as a likely cause.

The final issue in a negligence claim is whether the plaintiff suffered damages. The plaintiff is likely to make claims for the following compensatory damages: medical expenses, wages, future earning capacity, pain and suffering, emotional distress, loss of consortium, and change of life issues. Her potential award is mitigated by her medical recovery, by her improved personal relationships, and by the speculative nature of harm to her company. The Plaintiff will most likely try to build a case around her fear of seizures and the traumatic nature of a seizure. The doctor has said it is unlikely that the Plaintiff will have another seizure. We will need to demonstrate that her fear is not rational and that people in similar circumstances lead normal, seizure-free lives. The facts don't support a damage award exceeding the company's $10 million insurance reserve. Plaintiff may be asking for money to compensate for an unreasonable lifestyle. We probably want jurors who do not relate to the fancy lifestyle of both Darngood and the witness, Earle. Darngood was also making work style choices that may demonstrate an inappropriate work life not conducive to family values.

Defendants have three potential affirmative defenses to the negligence claim, which are: assumption of risk, contributory negligence, and comparative negligence. Under an implied assumption of risk defense, a plaintiff may be barred from recovery when an injury results from a danger of which plaintiff was aware and that plaintiff voluntarily encountered. Arguably, a person knows and agrees to assume the risk of crossing a street, especially when they don't look before crossing or cross against a red light. Under a contributory negligence defense, a plaintiff who is negligent and whose negligence contributes proximately to his injuries is totally barred from recovery. Arguably, the plaintiff failed to maintain proper lookout, and this failure was the cause of her injury. Finally, under a comparative negligence defense, the conduct on the part of the plaintiff that falls below the standard of conduct that Darngood should conform to for Darngood's own protection and is a legal contributing cause in bringing about the plaintiff's harm is only a partial bar to the plaintiff's recovery. The standard of conduct required by a pedestrian is to maintain proper lookout, which the plaintiff did not do here. Landers and PUDS can assert reasonable affirmative defenses, which may bar or mitigate the plaintiff's claim.

If it is determined that Landers was negligent, then PUDS is liable as well. Under the theory of respondeat superior, employers are vicariously liable for the torts of their employees when (1) the source of the injury at issue is related to duties of the employee; and (2) the tort occurs within the work-related limits of time and space. *Weiss v. Larson*, 633 Nita 2d 355 **(Year -5)**; *Fahrendorff v. North Homes, Inc.*, 632 Nita 2d 405 (Year -6). Foreseeability is an important factor in determining whether the act is related to the duties of employment. *Hagen v. Burmeister & Assoc., Inc.*, 633 Nita 2d 497 **(Year -5)**.

We are concerned that the jury may award larger damages because PUDS may be seen to have substantial funds, and it will be difficult to personalize the company. We can use Homer Picket to bring a human face to PUDS.

Here it is likely Landers was acting in the scope and course of employment when the accident occurred. Landers was driving a PUDS van for the purpose of making a PUDS' delivery. Moreover, PUDS should not have served alcohol at its holiday party because some of their drivers, Landers included, still needed to make deliveries.

Darngood v. Landers and PUDS, Plaintiff

CONCLUSION / RECOMMENDATIONS

This case, like other Nita pedestrian/driver cases, turns on witness credibility and fact interpretation. This case will be won based on the lawyer's advocacy skills. Our trial strategy should be the following: 1) bolster Landers's credibility by emphasizing Landers's honesty, excellent work history, and family history; 2) stress that the investigating officer, who was at the scene, determined there was a lack of witnesses and the witnesses' stories were conflicting; 3) emphasize that while life is sometimes tragic, in this situation for both parties, it doesn't necessarily mean someone is at fault; 4) demonstrate that Landers drove reasonably through the intersection using reasonable care under the circumstances; and 5) point out the plaintiff had a duty of care and demonstrate she didn't look before walking and was the only person in the intersection.

The biggest defense challenges are Landers's use of alcohol and the fact that the plaintiff was a pedestrian who was physically injured. There will be a bias in favor of finding fault against a driver when a pedestrian is injured. Also, if Landers is found liable for negligence, then PUDS will also be liable for negligence under the theory of respondeat superior.

We will always refer to the vehicle as a van, not a truck, and will describe the accident as Darngood stepping in front of the van, getting bumped, falling down, and hitting her head. She had bruises, but no cuts, broken bones, or torn clothing.

We will need to demonstrate that although Darngood has been changed, she can still lead a normal life and should not be compensated for a lifestyle of the "rich and famous."

APPENDIX G

SUMMARY OF CASES CITED

SUMMARY OF CASES CITED

D.M.S. v. Hair, 745 Nita 2d 637 (Year -2).

Alleged sexual abuse victim brought personal injury action against foster parent and foster care placement agency alleging that agency negligently hired, retained, and supervised foster parent, and that agency was responsible for foster parent's wrongful conduct under doctrine of respondeat superior. The District Court granted summary judgment to agency. Victim appealed. The Court of Appeals affirmed. Upon grant of victim's petition for review, the Supreme Court held that: (1) victim's action accrued, and six-year period enumerated in delayed discovery statute began to run, when victim reached his eighteenth birthday, and (2) victim's respondeat superior claim was governed by six-year limitations period in delayed discovery statute, rather than two-year limitations period for battery actions.

Fahrendorff v. North Homes, Inc., 632 Nita 2d 405 (Year -6).

Teen was sexually assaulted at a teen crisis center program by the coordinator. Teen's mother brought suit against employer asserting liability for various tort claims based on the doctrine of respondeat superior. The trial court granted summary judgment for the employer stating that employee was not acting within the scope and course of his employment. The Court of Appeals affirmed. The Supreme Court reversed and remanded to resolve a factual dispute. In particular there was factual dispute whether the employee's conduct was foreseeable.

Hagen v. Burmeister & Assoc., Inc., 633 Nita 2d 497 (Year -5).

An employee sued a prior employer to establish employee's ability to contact prior insurance consumers. The prior employer counterclaimed with tortuous interference with contract. The prior employer's claim was based on the theory of respondeat superior. The Supreme Court reversed the Court of Appeals' determination that the prior employee's conduct was foreseeable.

Hamry v. Zebo, 532 Nita 2d 281 (Year -18).

Motorist brought action for personal injuries she sustained when she struck disabled truck in traveled portion of road. The District Court ruled that defendant was negligent as matter of law, entered judgment on jury verdict in plaintiff's favor, and denied defendant's motions for new trial and judgment notwithstanding the verdict. Defendant appealed. The Court of Appeals held that: (1) driver of disabled pickup truck, who waited for roughly thirty minutes to attempt to push truck off road notwithstanding presence of two passengers in pickup who could have assisted him in efforts, was negligent as matter of law, and (2) evidence of defendant's alcohol consumption shortly before accident was admissible.

Metropolitan Employees Ret. Fund v. Anson-Williams Co., 619 Nita 2d 568 (Year -12).

Pension fund brought action against a securities broker for breach of fiduciary duty, negligence, and violation of Nita securities laws in connection with broker's sale of securities to fund. The District Court granted broker's motion for summary judgment, and pension fund appealed. The Court of Appeals affirmed in part and reversed in part, and review was granted. The Supreme Court held that: (1) pension plan did not have general unsuitability claim against broker under Nita securities fraud statute; (2) broker did not violate regulation imposing duty to obtain information concerning customer's financial situation and other securities holdings; and (3) Nita Securities Act regulations prohibiting recommendation of unsuitable securities and prohibiting charging of excessive markups did not create new standard of care for brokers.

Peterson v. Egg, 395 Nita 2d 715 (Year -26).

Passenger who was injured in an automobile accident appealed from a judgment of the District Court in her action to recover damages for personal injuries she suffered as a result of the accident. The Supreme Court held that: (1) passenger established reasonable certainty of future medical expenses by fair preponderance of the evidence, including testimony of orthopedic surgeon that over 50 percent of group of 100 individuals with knee x-rays identical to those of passenger would eventually undergo knee reconstructive surgery and that passenger's degenerate knee condition would progress to the point at which she would probably seek pain relief afforded by knee reconstructive surgery; therefore, trial court erred when it refused to instruct jury on future knee reconstructive surgery and attendant future medical expenses; and (2) future pain and suffering and future diminished earning capacity were so inextricably tied to future surgery and its attendant expenses that new trial on issue of special and general damages would be required in light of trial court's failure to instruct on future surgery.

Rowen v. May, 802 Nita 2d 33 (Year -1).

Motorist brought personal injury action against driver of vehicle that rear-ended her vehicle, and driver eventually conceded he bore liability for accident. Following a jury trial on damages only, the District Court entered judgment awarding plaintiff $24,000 and denied defendant's motion for a new trial. Defendant appealed. The Court of Appeals reversed and remanded. Plaintiff appealed. The Supreme Court held that: (1) burden of proof remains on the plaintiff in cases involving aggravation of a preexisting injury; (2) civil pattern jury instruction providing that "[i]f you cannot separate damages caused by the preexisting disability or medical condition from those caused by the accident, then [defendant] is liable for all the damages," misstates Nita law when it is given to jury in cases involving one defendant and aggravation of a preexisting injury; and (3) total effect of erroneous instruction could not be determined, and thus defendant was entitled to a new trial on damages.

Thom v. Mullett, 188 Nita 2d 98 (Year -48).

Action by pedestrian who was struck by automobile while crossing intersection controlled by automatic stop and go traffic signals. The District Court rendered judgment for defendants and denied pedestrian's motion for new trial; pedestrian appealed. The Supreme Court held that where there was evidence that it had been raining or drizzling at time of accident; that pedestrian might have been running as she crossed intersection; that, while light had been green for pedestrian it changed to red as she started to cross; and that she was wearing dark clothes, questions of negligence of driver and pedestrian's contributory negligence were for jury.

Weiss v. Larson, 633 Nita 2d 355 (Year -5).

An employee of a commercial furniture moving company is acting within the scope of employment even if the employee at the time of an accident violates a traffic violation and is found at fault in a personal injury motor vehicle accident. The employer is liable for the actions of the employee and subsequent consequences under the well-established doctrine of respondeat superior.

Darngood v. Landers and PUDS, Plaintiff

APPENDIX H
JURY INSTRUCTIONS AND
SPECIAL VERDICT FORM

DARNGOOD V. LANDERS AND PICKET UP DELIVERY SERVICES

PART I

PRELIMINARY JURY INSTRUCTIONS

(Given Prior to the Evidence)

The following jury instructions state general principles that may apply to this case and may be used at the discretion of the trial judge.

A. Introduction

You have been selected as jurors and have taken an oath to well and truly try this cause. This trial will last one day.

During the process of the trial there will be periods of time when the court recesses. During those periods of time you must not talk about this case among yourselves or with anyone else.

During the trial, do not talk to any of the parties, their lawyers, or any of the witnesses.

If any attempt is made by anyone to talk to you concerning the matters here under consideration you should report the fact to the court immediately.

You should keep an open mind. You should not form or express an opinion during the trial and should reach no conclusion in this case until you have heard all of the evidence, the arguments of counsel, and the final instructions as to the law, which will be given to you by the court.

B. Conduct of the Trial

First, the attorneys will have an opportunity to make opening statements. These statements are not evidence and should be considered only as a preview of what the attorneys expect the evidence will be.

Following the opening statements, witnesses will be called to testify. They will be placed under oath and questioned by the attorneys. Documents and other tangible exhibits may also be received as evidence. If an exhibit is given to you to examine, you should examine it carefully, individually, and without any comment.

It is the right of counsel to object when testimony or other evidence is offered that the attorney believes is not admissible.

When the court sustains an objection to a question, the jurors must disregard the question and the answer if one has been given, and draw no inference from the question or answer or speculate as to what the witness would have said if permitted to answer. Evidence stricken from the record must likewise be disregarded.

When the court sustains an objection to any evidence, the jurors must disregard such evidence.

When the court overrules an objection to any evidence, the jurors must not give such evidence any more weight than if the objection had not been made.

When the evidence is completed, the attorneys will make final statements. These final statements are not evidence but are given to assist you in evaluating the evidence. The attorneys are also permitted to argue, to attempt to persuade you to a particular verdict. You may accept or reject those arguments as you see fit.

Finally, just before you retire to consider your verdict, you will receive further instructions on the law that applies to this case.

Darngood v. Landers and PUDS, Plaintiff

PART II

FINAL JURY INSTRUCTIONS

(Given at Conclusion of Evidence)

A. Introduction

Members of the jury, the evidence and arguments in this case have been completed, and you will now receive instructions concerning the law.

The law applicable in this case is stated in these instructions, and it is your duty to follow the instructions and law. The order in which the instructions are given is not significant. You must not single out certain instructions and disregard others.

It is your duty to determine the facts and to determine them only from the evidence in this case. You are to apply the law to the facts and in this way decide the case. You must not be governed or influenced by sympathy or prejudice for or against any party in this case. Your verdict must be based on evidence and not upon speculation, guess, or conjecture.

From time to time it has been the duty of the court to rule on the admissibility of evidence. You must not concern yourselves with the reasons for these rulings. You should disregard questions and exhibits that were withdrawn or to which objections were sustained.

You should also disregard testimony and exhibits that the court has refused or stricken.

The evidence that you should consider consists only of the testimony of the witnesses and the exhibits the court has received.

Any evidence that was received for a limited purpose should not be considered by you for any other purpose.

You should consider all the evidence in the light of your own observations and experiences in life.

Neither these instructions nor any ruling or remark indicate any opinion as to the facts or as to what your verdict should be.

B. Opening Statement/Closing Arguments

Opening statements are made by the attorneys to acquaint you with the facts they expect to prove. Closing arguments are made by the attorneys to discuss the facts and circumstances in the case and should be confined to the evidence and to reasonable inferences to be drawn therefrom. Neither opening statements nor closing arguments are evidence, and any statement or argument made by the attorneys that is not based on the evidence should be disregarded.

C. Credibility of Witnesses

You are the sole judge of the credibility of the witnesses and of the weight to be given the testimony of each. In determining what credit is to be given any witness you may take into account his ability and opportunity to observe; his manner and appearance while testifying; any interest, bias, or prejudice he may have; the reasonableness of his testimony considered in the light of all the evidence; and any other factors that bear on the believability and weight of the witness's testimony.

D. Expert Witnesses (When Applicable)

You have heard evidence in this case from witnesses who have testified as experts. The law allows experts to express opinion on subjects involving their special knowledge, training and skill, experience or research; but while their opinions are allowed to be given, it is entirely within the province of the jury to determine what weight shall be given their testimony. Jurors are not bound by the testimony of experts; their testimony is to be weighed as that of any other witness.

E. Direct and Circumstantial Evidence

The law recognizes two kinds of evidence—direct and circumstantial. Direct evidence proves a fact directly—that is, the evidence by itself, if true, establishes the fact. Circumstantial evidence is the proof of facts or circumstances that give rise to a reasonable inference of other facts—that is, circumstantial evidence proves a fact indirectly in that it follows from other facts or circumstances according to common experience and observations in life. An eyewitness is a common example of direct evidence, while human footprints are circumstantial evidence that a person was present.

The law makes no distinction between direct and circumstantial evidence as to degree of proof required, and each should be considered according to whatever weight or value it may have. All of the evidence should be considered and evaluated by you in arriving at your verdict.

Darngood v. Landers and PUDS, Plaintiff

PART III

PROPOSED AND OPTIONAL JURY INSTRUCTIONS

A. Claims and Defenses

The court will now instruct you on the claims and defenses of each party and the law governing the case. You must arrive at your verdict by unanimous vote, applying the law, as you are now instructed, to the facts as you find them to be.

The plaintiff is Helen Darngood. Defendants are Mel Landers and Picket Up Delivery Services. The plaintiff in this case claims damages from the defendants.

The parties agree on the following:

1. The accident occurred on the early evening of December 23, _____ (Year -2), on the corner of Seventh Street and Smith Avenue.

2. Helen Darngood was in the crosswalk on the corner of Seventh Street and Smith Avenue, traveling from north to south.

3. Mel Landers was driving a Picket Up Delivery van on Smith Avenue from east to west and was acting in the scope of employment while working for Picket Up Delivery Services at the time of the accident.

Denials

Plaintiff denies:

- Contributory Negligence

Defendant Mel Landers denies:

- Negligence

Defendant Picket Up Delivery Services denies:

- Negligence

B. Direct Cause

A direct cause is a cause that has a substantial part in bringing about the injury. There may be more than one direct cause of an injury. When the effects of negligent conduct of each of two or more persons actively work at substantially the same time to cause the injury, without either being a superseding cause, each may be a direct cause of the injury.

C. Negligence and Reasonable Care

The mere fact that a collision has happened does not of itself mean that anyone has been negligent.

A person may assume that every other person will use reasonable care and will obey the law until the contrary reasonably appears.

Negligence is the failure to use reasonable care. Reasonable care is that care that a reasonable person would use under like circumstances. Negligence is the doing of something that a reasonable person would not do, or the failure to do something a reasonable person would do, under like circumstances.

The violation of a duty owed another to use reasonable care is negligence. The duty of reasonable care may include, among other things:

1. The duty of every person using a public roadway as a driver of a vehicle or a pedestrian to maintain a reasonable lookout.

2. The duty of a driver of a vehicle to keep driver's vehicle under control.

Whether or not a duty has been violated depends upon the risks of the situation, the dangers known or reasonably to have been foreseen, and all of the then-existing circumstances.

D. Contributory Fault

Contributory fault does not bar recovery in an action by any person or the person's legal representative to recover damages for fault resulting in death, in injury to person or property, or in economic loss, if the contributory fault was not greater than the fault of the person against whom recovery is sought. The jury shall determine the amount of damages and percentage of fault attributable to each party.

E. Damages

The term "damages" means a sum of money that will fairly compensate a person injured. Damages may be recovered for past and future harm. However, it must be proved such future harm is reasonably certain to occur.

A party seeking damages must prove the nature, extent, duration, and consequences of harm.

In determining the amount of damages to parties you are to consider the following:

1. Present and future physical and emotional damages.

2. The value of lost earnings and the possible loss of future earnings. If future earning capacity has been destroyed or reduced by termination, you may determine the present cash value of such loss or reduction of future earning capacity considering the age, health, skill, training, experience, and industry of the party.

3. Whether the damages or injuries are temporary or permanent.

F. Burden of Proof

In order to answer any question "yes," the greater weight of the evidence must support such an answer, otherwise you should answer the question "no." Greater weight of the evidence means that all of the evidence by whomever produced must lead you to believe it is more likely that the claim is true than not true. If the evidence does not lead you to believe it is more likely that the claim is true than not true, then the claim has not been proved by the greater weight of the evidence.

The greater weight of the evidence does not necessarily mean the greater number of witnesses or the greater volume of testimony. Any believable evidence may be a sufficient basis to prove a fact.

A party seeking damages must prove the nature, extent, duration, and consequences of harm.

In determining the amount of damages to both parties you are to consider the following:

1. The physical pain, disability, disfigurement, and mental suffering experienced and is reasonably certain to experience in the future as a result of the injuries;

2. The value of lost earnings and the possible loss of future earnings. If future earning capacity has been destroyed or reduced by injuries, you may determine the present cash value of such loss or reduction of future earning capacity considering the age, health, skill, training, experience, and industry of the party, and whether the injuries are temporary or permanent.

Darngood v. Landers and PUDS, Plaintiff

G. Concluding Instruction

The court did not in any way and does not by these instructions give or intimate any opinions as to what has or has not been proven in this case, or as to what are or are not the facts of the case.

No one of these instructions states all of the law applicable, but all of them must be taken, read, and considered together as they are connected with and related to each other as a whole.

You must not be concerned with the wisdom of any rule of law. Regardless of any opinions you may have as to what the law ought to be, it would be a violation of your sworn duty to base a verdict upon any other view of the law than that given in the instructions of the court.

SPECIAL VERDICT FORM

STATE OF NITA   **DISTRICT COURT**

COUNTY OF DARROW   **SECOND JUDICIAL DISTRICT**

_____

HELEN DARNGOOD,

          Plaintiff,

          v.   **SPECIAL VERDICT**

MEL LANDERS, AN INDIVIDUAL,

AND PICKET UP DELIVERY SERVICES,

A NITA CORPORATION

          Defendants.

_____

We, the Jury, in the above-entitled matter, make the following Findings of Fact:

Question 1   Were the Defendants Mel Landers and Picket Up Delivery Services negligent in connection with this accident?

                Yes _____   No _____

Question 2   If your answer to Question 1 was "yes," then answer this question:

            Was such negligence a direct cause of the accident?

                Yes _____   No _____

Question 3   Was the Plaintiff negligent in connection with this accident?

                Yes _____   No _____

Question 4   If your answer to Question 3 was "yes," then answer this question:

Was such negligence a direct cause of the collision?

Yes _____   No _____

Question 5   If you answered "yes" to Questions 1, 2, 3 and 4, then answer this question:

Taking all of the negligence that contributed as a direct cause to the accident being 100%, what percentage or portion thereof do you attribute to:

Defendant Landers and Picket Up Delivery Services   _____%

Plaintiff   _____%

TOTAL   100%

Regardless of your answers to the previous Questions, you must answer Question 6.

Question 6   What sum of money will fairly and adequately compensate Plaintiff for all damages resulting from this accident?

Economic $_____

Emotional/Physical $_____

EXHIBITS LIST
[Exhibits Located on CD]

Exhibit 1:   Collective Bargaining Agreement between Picket Up Delivery Services and IATW
   (Witnesses: Mel Landers, Perry Reinhart, Homer Picket)

Exhibit 2:   Picket Up Delivery Services Special Rule—Traffic Violation Policy: B(1)
   (Witnesses: Mel Landers, Perry Reinhart, Homer Picket)

Exhibit 3:   Memo from Homer Picket to Employee (Landers) File
   (Witnesses: Homer Picket and Mel Landers)

Exhibit 4:   Letter of Reprimand from Juliette Nelson-Picket to Mel Landers
   (Witnesses: Mel Landers, Perry Reinhart)

Exhibit 5:   PUDS Van Specifications
   (By Stipulation—All Parties)

Exhibit 6:   Picture of Mussel Pot
   (Witness: Cooper Earle)

Exhibit 7:   Photograph of Stop and Walk Signals
   (Witnesses: Helen Darngood, Cooper Earle, Mel Landers)

Exhibit 8:   Speed Calculation
   (By Stipulation—All Parties)

Exhibit 9:   Photographs of PUDS Uniform Shirt (Front and Back)
   (Witnesses: Cooper Earle, Mel Landers, Perry Reinhart)

Exhibit 10:   Photograph of Downtown Nita City—Looking North on Seventh Street from Grand Avenue
   (Witnesses: Helen Darngood, Cooper Earle, Mel Landers)

Exhibit 11:   Accident Diagram With Picket Up Delivery Services Van
   (Witnesses: Mel Landers, Helen Darngood, Cooper Earle)

Exhibit 12:   Accident Diagram Without Picket Up Delivery Services Van
   (Witnesses: Mel Landers, Helen Darngood, Cooper Earle)

Exhibit 13:   Alcohol Influence Report
   (By Stipulation—All Parties)

Exhibit 14:   Intoxilyzer Test Record
   (By Stipulation—All Parties)

Exhibit 15:   Alcohol Impairment Charts
   (By Stipulation—All Parties)

Exhibit 16:   Helen Darngood's Resignation Letter
   (Witness: Helen Darngood)

Exhibit 17:   Expert Medical Report, C.R. Strickland, MD
   (By Stipulation—All Parties)

Exhibit 18:   Manual for the Wheeled Vehicle Driver—Departments of Army and Air Force
   (By Stipulation—All Parties)

LEARNING
MATERIALS

PLANNING GUIDE AND CHECKLIST

The planning guide and checklist is provided to help the preparation of legal substance and presentation. It provides the basis for the preparation of more detailed planning.

Section 1. General

A. Professional Responsibility
- Pervades all exercise activities
- Role of attorney
  - Fact finding
  - Evaluating evidence
  - Analyzing applicable law, legal elements, and precedent
  - Developing legal theories
  - Applying applicable law to specific facts
  - Assessing strengths and weaknesses of client's case
  - Assessing strengths and weaknesses of opponent's case
  - Presenting options
  - Evaluating and prioritizing options with client input
  - Counseling client
  - Negotiating an advantageous result for client
  - Advocating zealously for client
  - Drafting and reviewing documents
  - Keeping client reasonably informed
  - Advising client of legal rights, obligations, implications, and consequences
- Attorney-client privilege
- Confidentiality
  - Model Rule of Professional Conduct 1.6: Confidentiality of Information
- Conflict of interest
  - Model Rule of Professional Conduct 1.7: Conflict of Interest: Current Clients
  - Model Rule of Professional Conduct 1.8: Conflict of Interest: Current Clients: Specific Rules
  - Model Rule of Professional Conduct 1.9: Duties to Former Clients
  - Model Rule of Professional Conduct 1.10: Imputation of Conflicts of Interest: General Rule
  - Model Rule of Professional Conduct 1.11: Special Conflicts of Interest for Former and Current Government Officers and Employees
  - Model Rule of Professional Conduct 1.12: Former Judge, Arbitrator, Mediator, or Other Third-Party Neutral
- Authority to settle
  - Model Rule of Professional Conduct 1.2: Scope of Representation and Allocation of Authority Between Client and Lawyer
    - 62(a) "A lawyer shall abide by a client's decision whether to settle a matter."

B. Client/Witness Interviews
- Preparation
  - Confirm time and location with client/witness
  - Have client/witness bring all relevant documents or other evidence
  - Develop a basic understanding of client's/witness's situation
  - Conduct preliminary research and investigation

- Rapport
  - Know client's/witness's name and preferred form of address
  - Make client/witness feel at ease
  - Establish trust
- Efficient factual inquiry
  - Elicit all facts, favorable and unfavorable
  - Find out what client/witness needs and hopes to accomplish
  - Focus on pertinent issues; avoid tangential, nonrelevant inquiry
- Anticipate and analyze pertinent legal issues
  - Statutes of limitations
  - Evaluate all possible causes of action and remedies
  - Eliminate frivolous or marginal theories
- Assess client's case
  - Be realistic
  - Compare probable outcomes with client's expectations and needs
  - Consider emotional and financial impact of contemplated action
  - Estimate time required to effectively represent client
- Reject client if necessary
  - Clearly explain reasons for rejection to client
  - Inform client of applicable statutes of limitations and filing deadlines
  - Encourage client to seek another opinion as soon as possible
  - Refer client
  - Confirm rejection by e-mail and letter, clearly stating reasons and deadlines
- Develop preliminary strategy with client
  - Negotiation
  - Mediation
  - Arbitration
  - Litigation
- Have client sign all necessary documents
  - Representation agreement
  - Information releases (school, medical, workplace)
  - Waivers

C. Representation Agreements
- Specifically tailored to the identity and needs of the individual client
- Client is clearly identified
- Scope of the representation is clearly defined
- Clearly defining allocation of authority
- Responsibility for attorney fees, costs, and expenses is adequately explained
- Reasonable and customary fees, costs, and expenses are explained
- Billing procedures are clearly stated
- Attorney responsibilities are adequately defined
- Client responsibilities are adequately defined
- Appropriate termination provisions are included
- Agreement overall complies with local Rules of Professional Conduct
- Coherent grammar
- Proofread

- Client can easily understand agreement
- Reviewed and signed by client

D. Fees
- Abide by applicable Rules of Professional Conduct
  o *See* Model Rule of Professional Conduct 1.5: Fees
  o Give client a simple memorandum or copy of customary fee agreement including:
    – General nature of legal services
    – The basis
    – Rate or total amount of fees (reasonable and customary)
    – Whether and to what extent fees are subject to change
    – Whether and to what extent client is responsible for costs, expenses, or disbursements
    – The responsibilities of the attorney and client under the agreement
- Contingency
  o Must be in writing, stating method by which fee is determined and percentage
  o Conforms to legal limitations
    – Ceiling on percent
    – Required alternative fee offering
  o Clearly explained to client
  o Including how disbursements and costs affect contingency fee and client's recovery
- Straight time (hourly)
- Price per project
- Billable time
  o Client and witness interviews
  o Phone calls
  o E-mail
  o Consultation with other attorneys
  o Research
  o Prepare exhibits and schedule
  o Legal assistant/law clerk time
  o Drafting/reviewing documents
  o Depositions
  o Filing court documents
  o Negotiation
  o Mediation
  o Arbitration
  o Court time/appearances
- Billing procedures
  o Accurate timekeeping
  o Itemized statements
  o Clear explanation of payment terms
  o Regular billing cycle

E. Costs and Expenses
- Filing and other court fees
- Notary/service of process fees
- Investigation costs
- Expert witnesses

- Fees and travel
- Court reporters
- Exhibits
- Travel and mileage
- Phone charges
- Postage
- Copies
- Couriers/service fees

F. Sources of Law
- Statutes
  o Specific to issues
  o Source of substantive law
  o Time limitations on claims—*see* local statutes for applicable law
- Case Law
  o Source of substantive law
  o Interprets the elements of a claim
- Other Sources
  o Treatises/hornbooks/textbooks
  o Practice guides/CLE materials
  o Digests and annotations
  o Looseleaf services
  o Specialized publications and periodicals/law review articles
  o Legal dictionaries and encyclopedias
  o Electronic services/CD-ROM
  o Consultation with others
  o Administrative materials
  o Briefs

G. Rules of Evidence and Procedure
- The rules of evidence and procedure may vary—check with judge/arbitrator
- For persuasive purposes, foundations for testimony and exhibits should be presented even if not required
- Check local rules and practice
  o Elements of the claim
  o Sufficiency of evidence
  o Burden of proof
  o Order of evidence
  o Validity of claims
  o Limitation of remedies
  o Damages/Measure/Mitigation
  o Admissibility of potential evidence, testimony, and exhibits
    – Federal Rule of Evidence 105: Limited Admissibility
    – Federal Rule of Evidence 404: Character Evidence Not Admissible to Prove Conduct; Exceptions; Other Crimes
    – Federal Rule of Evidence 802: Hearsay Rule
    – Federal Rule of Evidence 804: Hearsay Exceptions; Declarant Unavailable
    –

- Relevancy of potential evidence, testimony and exhibits
  o Federal Rule of Evidence 104(a): Questions of Admissibility Generally
  o Federal Rule of Evidence 104(b): Relevancy Conditioned on Fact
  o Federal Rule of Evidence 401: Definition of "Relevant Evidence"
  o Federal Rule of Evidence 402: Relevant Evidence Generally Admissible; Irrelevant Evidence Inadmissible
  o Federal Rule of Evidence 403: Exclusion of Relevant Evidence on Grounds of Prejudice, Confusion, or Waste of Time
- Objections to potential evidence, testimony, and exhibits
  o Mischaracterization of evidence
  o Misstatement of facts
  o Irrelevant question
  o Misleading or confusing question
  o Outside the scope of rebuttal argument
  o Multiple or compound questions
  o Leading question
  o Improper impeachment
- Local Rules of General Practice/Civil Procedure
  o Primary source of procedural law at trial level
  o Venue-specific rules
- Litigation timing
- Pleading and motion requirements
  o Federal Rule of Civil Procedure 4: Summons
  o Federal Rule of Civil Procedure 4.1: Serving of Other Process
  o Federal Rule of Civil Procedure 5: Serving and Filing Pleadings and Other Papers
  o Federal Rule of Civil Procedure 7: Pleadings Allowed; Form of Motions and Other Papers
  o Federal Rule of Civil Procedure 7.1: Disclosure Statement
  o Federal Rule of Civil Procedure 8: General Rules of Pleading
  o Federal Rule of Civil Procedure 10: Form of Pleadings
  o Federal Rule of Civil Procedure 11: Signing Pleadings, Motions, and Other Papers; Representations to Court; Sanctions
  o Federal Rule of Civil Procedure 15: Amended and Supplemental Pleadings
- Discovery options and limitations
  o Federal Rule of Civil Procedure 16: Pretrial Conferences; Scheduling; Management
  o Federal Rule of Civil Procedure 33: Interrogatories to Parties
  o Federal Rule of Civil Procedure 34: Production of Documents, Electronically Stored Information, and Tangible Things, or Entering upon Land, for Inspection and Other Purposes
  o Federal Rule of Civil Procedure 35: Physical and Mental Examinations
  o Federal Rule of Civil Procedure 36: Requests for Admission
  o Federal Rule of Civil Procedure 37: Failure to Make Disclosures or Cooperate in Discovery; Sanctions
- Pretrial responsibilities
  o Federal Rule of Civil Procedure 3: Commencing an Action
  o Federal Rule of Civil Procedure 4: Summons
  o Federal Rule of Civil Procedure 5: Serving and Filing Pleadings and Other Papers
  o Federal Rule of Civil Procedure 7: Pleadings Allowed; Form of Motions and Other Papers
  o Federal Rule of Civil Procedure 7.1: Disclosure Statement
  o Federal Rule of Civil Procedure 8: General Rules of Pleading

  o Federal Rule of Civil Procedure 10: Form of Pleadings
  o Federal Rule of Civil Procedure 11: Signing Pleadings, Motions, and Other Papers; Representations to the Court; Sanctions
  o Federal Rule of Civil Procedure 15: Amended and Supplemental Pleadings
  o Federal Rule of Civil Procedure 16: Pretrial Conferences; Scheduling; Management

H. Practical Considerations
- Internal memos
  - Used as a preliminary internal analysis of the strengths and weaknesses of the case
  - Not to exceed reasonable page length
  - Appropriate margin, font, and line-spacing adjustments
  - Coherent overall, paragraph, and sentence structure
  - Proofread and checked for misspelling
  - Pertinent issues clearly identified
  - Applicable procedural and substantive law identified
  - Applicable law applied to specific case facts
  - Neutral assessment as to how the pertinent issues may be resolved
  - Appropriate substance and level of analysis for intended audience
  - Easy to read and informative
- Demand for payment on policy (if insurance company is involved)
  - Information disclosure
  - Deadline for responses
  - Negotiations
- Pleadings
  - Summons and Complaint
    - Short and plain statement showing pleader is entitled to the specific relief demanded
    - Filed within statute of limitations
    - Appropriate jurisdiction and venue, service of process
    - Proper format, caption, acknowledgments, and signatures
    - Clearly identifies the court and parties'/attorney's name and address
    - States a valid cause of action necessary elements
    - Alleges facts sufficient to support prima facie claims
    - Timely served on court and opposing party
  - Answer and Counterclaim
    - Short and plain defenses to each claim
    - Admit/deny each allegation
    - Appropriate challenges to sufficiency of process and service of process
    - Must state if not enough information to admit/deny
    - Appropriate challenges to jurisdiction and venue
    - Appropriate challenges to stated claims
    - Proper format, caption, acknowledgments, and signatures
    - Answer raises applicable avoidance or affirmative defenses
    - Answer adequately responds to all allegations of the complaint
    - Counterclaim states a valid cause of action/necessary elements
    - Counterclaim alleges facts sufficient to support prima facie claims
    - Counterclaim clearly specifies and requests appropriate relief
    - Timely served on court and opposing party
    -

- o Reply to Counterclaim
  - – Appropriate challenges to stated counterclaims
  - – Proper format, caption, acknowledgments, and signatures
  - – Raises applicable affirmative defenses
  - – Adequately responds to all allegations of counterclaim
  - – Timely served on court and opposing party
- o Motions
  - – Failure to state a claim upon which relief can be granted
  - – Challenges to jurisdiction and venue
  - – Challenges to sufficiency of process and service of process
- o Pleading Deadlines
- o Discovery Deadlines
- o Pretrial motions
  - – Dispositive
  - – Nondispositive
- o Pretrial settlement conference/hearing

Section 2. Negotiation

A. Negotiation Preparation
- • Preliminary Negotiation Preparation
  - o Initial client meeting—derive basic factual picture
  - o Alternate questions—open, follow-up, closed, leading, summary
  - o Convey expectations and recognition of full, relevant disclosure
  - o Anticipate and overcome etiquette barriers (e.g., talk of trauma, medical problems)
  - o Gather information—funnel, chronological order, quietly persist, prove, re-create events
  - o Review conflicts, nature/scope of representation
  - o Maintain normal client-attorney relations, if client mentally or physically disabled
  - o Decision making—lawyer-centered or collaborative
  - o Decide attorney role(s)—draftsman, agent, negotiator, advocate, spokesperson
  - o Obtain client objectives and prioritize
- • Strategy
  - o Style—working with client: directive or facilitating, broad v. narrow focus
  - o Goals—problem resolution considering any future relations
  - o Research facts and law
  - o Plan and prioritize arguments and evidentiary support
  - o Anticipate counterarguments
  - o Concessions
  - o Worst Alternative to a Negotiated Agreement (WATNA)
  - o Likely and Best Alternative to a Negotiated Agreement (LATNA, BATNA)
  - o Value of case, minimum/maximum ranges, remedies, aim high
  - o Liability, elements, special damages, insurance coverage, past verdicts
  - o Develop multiple, creative options
  - o Discuss nonlegal (psychological, social, economic, and moral) options, pros/cons
  - o Discuss legal options—best, likely, and worst consequences (percent probability of each)
  - o Set flexible time allowed for negotiation and deadline(s)
  - o Communicate logistical requirements, concerns
  - o Confer—who is permitted at negotiation?
  - o Confirm prior:

- authority to settle
- attendees
- agenda
- format
- method(s) of recordation
- publicity parameters
- confidentiality
  o Inventory, classify, and compare both sides' needs, interests, and objectives
  o Outline other's potential gains and losses
- Style Decision
  o Effective competitive negotiation style:
    - high opening demands
    - few concessions
    - positions related to interests
    - exaggeration
    - threats
    - aggression
  o Alternatively, effective cooperative negotiation style:
    - high opening demands
    - rational, logical persuasion
    - ours, theirs, and shared interests
    - objective criteria
    - fairness
    - trusting open exchanges
    - concessions to demonstrate good faith
    - realistic and analytical
- Negotiation Location and Arrangements
  o Make physical arrangements
  o Decide on beneficial psychological environment
  o Neutral site, or any reason to allow one party to host, advantages/ disadvantages

B. The Negotiation
  - Pay attention to non-negotiation conversation
  - Establish rapport
    o Facilitate open communication to net valuable information
    o Avoid religion, politics, personal, or sensitive subjects
  - Nonverbal behaviors
    o Observe nonverbal signals
    o Gauge eye contact for honesty, confidence, effect of communication
    o Watch facial expression, posture, and gestures
    o Check for surprising nonverbals
  - Listen
    o To acquire previously undisclosed information
    o Recognize interests, needs and fears
    o Evaluate counterpart's position
    o Actively listen, reflect, paraphrase, clarify interests and positions
    o Acknowledge hostility, blame, nondefensiveness (e.g., "I see you are upset, so what *do you feel* is a fair solution that we might accept?")

- Information Protection
    - Judiciously use "blocking techniques" to protect sensitive information
    - Ignore question
    - Declare question off limits (e.g., attorney-client privilege)
    - Answer a question with a question (evade by seeking clarification or elaboration)
    - Under/overanswering (generally to a specific question or conversely)
    - Answer honestly but incompletely
    - Beneficially reframe
    - Answer a different question than the one asked (e.g., "I understand you want to know . . .")
    - Answer a recently asked question again
- Communication
    - Convince opposing parties to change their resistance point by a cost-benefit summary
    - Frame options in reference to negotiator's objectives, as gain to other
    - Dissuade rejection, solely from "reactive devaluation" of other's offer
    - Reasonable, analytical, realistic, and rational
- Communicating offers and concessions
    - Briefly (to reduce counterpart's response time)
    - Specifically address conflict areas
    - Justify with objective reasons
    - Clearly state solutions, remedies, damage figures
- Reacting to offers
    - React immediately to an inadequate offer
    - Avoid bidding against yourself—ask opposing side how much better the offer has to be
    - React strongly to outrageous offers
    - Remain silent as long as possible, until the other speaks
    - State that offer appears acceptable, but final approval must be made by someone else
- Assessing negotiating competence and effectiveness
    - Outcome measures of effectiveness
    - Obtained profit-maximizing amount(s) and/or desired outcome in settlement
    - Reached agreement considering all relevant information and arguments
    - Compromised and conceded only what you had decided in advance
    - New information was factored into your negotiation
    - Used the probable trial outcome as a baseline for evaluation
    - Accurately estimated the value of particular items to the other side
    - Able to reconcile style, strategy, and acceptability of offers with your client
    - Process handled cost-effectively in terms of time, energy, and money
    - If applicable, preservation of relationship to facilitate compliance, long-term relations
- Post-Negotiation Self-Analysis
    - Decided in advance on style and strategy, yet remained flexible
    - Analyzed the other side's style and strategy and adopted accordingly
    - Reassessed client's BATNA, WATNA after receiving any new information
    - Accurately estimated the value of case with appropriate minimum/maximum range
    - Set/accomplished goals
    - Set the desired tone
    - Controlled the agenda
    - Received sufficient information—clarification or elaboration
    - Did not reveal too much
    - Failed to reveal information that should have been revealed (misrepresentation/fraud)

- o Kept in mind that it is always an option to walk out
- o No agreement reached, was result appropriate in the context of this negotiation?
- o In case of deadlock what might have been done to break the deadlock?
- o Maximized a fair, reasonable settlement
- o What could have been done differently in this negotiation and why?
- Visual Aids
  - o If an indexed settlement brochure was used, were visual aids and factual history included to bolster credence, confidence, and preparedness?
  - o Were visual aids used tactfully to persuade, influence, and increase understanding?
  - o Does the cover letter have conditions for the aid's use, provide for its return, and limit its evidentiary use?

Section 3. Mediation

A. Mediation Preparation
- Preliminary Mediation Preparation
  - o Initial contacts—derive basic factual picture
  - o Alternate questions—open, follow-up, closed, leading, summary
  - o Distinguish problem, positions, and interests (hidden agendas)
  - o Decide style—evaluative or facilitating, broad v. narrow focus
  - o Goals—problem resolution considering parties future relationship, if any
  - o Research facts and apply to pertinent law(s)
  - o Plan and prioritize agenda
  - o Anticipate arguments/counter arguments
  - o Concessions either side may need to make and reciprocal expectations
  - o Anticipate Worst Alternative to a Negotiated Agreement (WATNA)
  - o Anticipate Likely and Best Alternative to a Negotiated Agreement (LATNA, BATNA)
  - o Value the case, minimum/maximum ranges and creative remedies
  - o Send mediator a brief
  - o Expect but do not be overly concerned over high opening demands
  - o Develop many creative options
  - o Set flexible timeframe allowed for negotiation deadlines(s)
  - o Communicate logistical requirements and concerns
  - o Confer—who is permitted to attend
  - o Confirm immediately prior to mediation—formal authority to settle, attendees
- Procedure
  - o Consensus on ground rules, enforcement, just and fair standards/guides
  - o Be concrete, but flexible
  - o Identify issues
  - o Relate positions to interests (security, recognition, control, belonging)
  - o Rational, logical persuasion
  - o Identify conflicting, shared, and compatible interests
  - o Ensure buy-in by all parties participation
  - o Acknowledge, but do not react to emotional outbursts
  - o Recast attacks on mediator as an attack on the problem
  - o Dovetail differing interests
  - o Insist on objective criteria
  - o Agreement on fair standards/procedures

- o Expectations of fairness determined by party's perceptions
- o Facilitate trusting, open exchanges
- o Surrender something of value to the other side—give to get
- o If impasse, focus on positions, emotions; data, value, or relationship conflicts—continue mediation to later date as last resort
- o Keep caucusing as an option (straight talk)
- o Ask for concessions to demonstrate good faith, confront if none
- Mediation Location and Arrangements
  - o Make physical arrangements
  - o Decide on beneficial psychological environment
  - o Neutral site, or any reason to allow one party to host, advantages/disadvantages

B. The Mediation
- Pay attention to non-mediation conversation
  - o Establish rapport
  - o Facilitate open communication to net valuable information
  - o Avoid religion, politics, personal or sensitive subjects
- Nonverbal behaviors
  - o Observe nonverbal signals
  - o Telltale mannerisms and furtive expressions (example: fidgeting shows tension)
  - o Gauge eye contact for honesty, confidence, effect of communication
  - o Watch facial expression, posture, and gestures
  - o Check for surprising nonverbals (example: intentional false signals; pounding on desk)
  - o In diverse contexts—careful interpretation
- Listen
  - o To acquire previously undisclosed information
  - o Recognize interests, needs, and fears
  - o Evaluate counterpart's position by hearing others' point of view
  - o Ask for preferences
  - o Actively listen, reflect, paraphrase, and clarify interests and positions
  - o Acknowledge hostility, blame, defensiveness (e.g., I see you are upset)
  - o Do not accept a stalemate (e.g., so what *do you feel* is a fair solution you believe the other might accept?)
  - o Repeat opponent's proposals and concerns to clarify
- Information Protection
  - o Watch for "blocking techniques" and probe for relevant hidden information
    - – ignoring questions and moving to other's area of interest
    - – declaring questions off limits (e.g., attorney-client privilege or other plausible reason)
    - – answering a question with a question (evade by seeking clarification or elaboration)
    - – under/over-answering (generally to a specific question or conversely)
    - – answering honestly, but incompletely
    - – beneficially reframing to avoid revealing sensitive information
    - – answering different question than the one asked (e.g., I understand you want to know . . .)
    - – answering a recently asked question again
- Communication
  - o Reasonable, analytical, realistic, and rational
  - o Convince opposing side to change resistance by cost-benefit summary

- o Frame options as gain to other
- o Dissuade rejection form "reactive devaluation"
- Communicating offers and concessions
  - o Briefly stated (to decrease opposing party's reflection/ response time)
  - o Specifically addressed to conflict areas
  - o Relay justification with objective reasons
  - o Clearly stated solutions, remedies, damage figures
  - o Cleanly end final "niggling" (just one more thing) by other
  - o Finalize bargaining
  - o In drafting agreement, obtain buy-in on the language used
- Closure
  - o Trade concessions
  - o Give up enough to settle but not more
  - o If niggling, can agree by asking what they will give up in return
  - o Encourage movement toward closure
  - o Decide who drafts, what conditions to include, who monitors compliance
  - o Provisions for time extension, compliance standards, follow through
  - o Provide for future differences, back to mediation or arbitration
  - o Any exceptions to confidentiality
  - o Draft formal settlement agreement and execute (sign)
  - o Drafting fees agreed upon

Section 4. Discovery

A. Discovery
- Mandatory Disclosures
- Interrogatories (only to opposing parties)
  - o Proper citation and form (adequately inform of information requested)
  - o Do not exceed total number allowed (twenty-five absent court order or local rule)
  - o Appropriate set of instructions
  - o Appropriate definitions, if needed
  - o Reminder to opponent of duty to update answers
  - o Original questions, not copied from a book or set of forms
  - o Clear, precise, and direct questions
  - o Questions not vague, multiple, broad, or overly inclusive
  - o Focus on appropriate subject matter
  - o Comprehensive in overall scope, do not overlook important areas
  - o Not objectionable
  - o Pin down witness statements, recollections, opinions, or contentions
  - o Clarify or corroborate specific relevant facts
  - o Identify undiscovered witness, persons, documents, or other evidence (tangible things)
  - o Disprove the opponent's theory, and damage/relief claims
  - o Require answers that are nonevasive and complete
  - o Can be used with other methods of discovery
  - o Properly served on opposing party

B. Answers to Interrogatories
- See Federal Rules of Civil Procedure
  - o Objections to interrogatories

- o Failure to answer and evasive answers
- o Proper citation and form
- o Reasonable and rational interpretation of interrogatories
- o Appropriate and reasonable objections with specificity, executed by attorney
- o Appropriate, accurate, and complete answers to all interrogatories
- o Phrase answers to present best position of client
- Requests for production of documents
  - o Proper caption and form
  - o States time, place, and manner for production or inspection
  - o Defines documents in a broad sense, including all known media
  - o Reasonable number of requests
  - o Not objectionable, requiring reasonable compliance and disclosure
  - o Requests adequately defined, identified, or otherwise described
  - o Will produce all documents reasonably related to those requested
  - o Probes for additional sources of documents
  - o Properly served on opposing party
- Responses to requests for production of documents
  - o Reasonable compliance with nonobjectionable requests
  - o Appropriate method of compliance
  - o Seek protective order if necessary
  - o Properly served on opposing party
- Requests for admissions
  - o Proper caption and form
  - o Appropriate preface or instructions
  - o Appropriate definitions
  - o Short, simple precise requests
  - o No unnecessary adjectives, adverbs, or other characterizations
  - o Singularly listed in separately numbered paragraphs
  - o Not objectionable
  - o Call for unqualified responses
  - o Require reasonable admittance or denial of request
  - o Confirm key facts and contentions relating law to facts
  - o Establish the genuineness of documents
  - o Properly served on opposing party
- Responses to requests for admissions
  - o Proper caption and form
  - o Appropriate and reasonable objections
  - o Phrase answers to present best position of client
  - o Properly served on opposing party

C. Witness Depositions
- Prepare client before deposition
  - o Reduces witness's anxiety
  - o Address any new information that witness has learned
  - o Deposition procedures
  - o Different deposition styles
  - o Review documents with attorney in preparation for deposition
  - o Brief witness on applicable substantive law

- o Brief witness on privileged areas of the law
- o Explain objectionable questions
- o Explain that witness must respond to objectionable questions unless otherwise ordered not to respond
- o Outline of direct and expected cross-examinations
- o Demeanor and appearance to eventual fact finder
- o Instruct witness not to bring anything regarding the case to the deposition
- o Where and when to meet on the day of the deposition
- o Federal Rules of Evidence that govern expert/lay person testimony
- Questioning of Witness
  - o Focus on learning witness's version of the facts
  - o Begin with open ended questions
  - o Clarify information received
  - o Finish with closed questions suggesting answer to lock in testimony
  - o Continue a line of questioning until all information has been extracted/exhausted
- Expert witness depositions
  - o Prepare the witness before the deposition
    - – Deposition procedures
    - – Outline of direct and expected cross-examinations
    - – Demeanor and appearance to eventual fact finder
  - o Be ready to object when appropriate
  - o Direct examination
    - – Identify time, place, and individuals present
    - – Qualify the witness as an expert
    - – Properly lay foundation for and introduce any exhibits
    - – Elicit the basis for the expert's opinion
    - – Define technical terms
    - – Establish the opinion to a reasonable degree of certainty
    - – Introduce any harmful information
  - o Cross-examination
    - – Control the witness with leading questions
    - – Challenge the expert's qualifications
    - – Challenge the basis for the expert's opinions
    - – Challenge the expert's opinions
    - – Reinforce helpful information
  - o Redirect
    - – Rehabilitate expert's qualifications and opinions
    - – Clarify ambiguities and misstatements
    - – Reinforce helpful information

D. Defending Depositions
- Provide emotional comfort and support to client
- Preserve the record for anticipatory judge and jury
- Sit next to client
  - o Enables conferral with client
  - o Enables protection of client's interests
- Be prepared to object when appropriate

- o State objection for preservation
- o Relevancy
- o Prejudicial
- o Hearsay
- o Confusion of the issues
- o Competency
- o Question form
- o Foundation
- o Privilege
- Cross-examination
  - o Clarify previous answers
  - o Clarify answers (particularly where answers are subject to more than one interpretation)

Section 5. Motions/Oral Argument

A. Briefs
- Follow rules as to format and composition
  - o Does not exceed page limits
  - o Does not use margin, font, or line spacing adjustments to meet page limit
  - o Coherent overall, paragraph, and sentence structure
  - o Proofread and checked for misspelling
  - o Pertinent issues clearly identified
  - o Applicable procedural and substantive law identified
  - o Applicable law applied to specific case facts
- Table of contents
  - o Clearly label all parts of brief
  - o Provide accurate page references
- Table of authorities
  - o Separate authority by category
  - o List all authorities used in alphabetical order
- Legal issues
  - o Phrase issues concisely, in a way favorable to client
  - o Give the referee's answer to each issue
- Statement of the case
  - o State the procedural history of the case chronologically
  - o Provide citation to authorities, the transcript, and appendix
- Statement of facts
  - o Provide all facts necessary to support argument
  - o State facts in a neutral manner
  - o Present facts in a logical order
  - o Provide citation to the transcript and appendix
- Argument
  - o Use appropriate subheadings
  - o Outline standard of review
  - o Address each issue separately and thoroughly
  - o Apply applicable law to specific facts
  - o Provide compelling reasons why client should prevail

- Conclusion
  - Briefly recap reasons client should prevail
  - Ask for appropriate relief
- Appendix
  - Properly indexed and paginated
  - Contains all necessary exhibits and record excerpts

B. Oral Argument
  - Obey all court rules
  - Proper appearance and demeanor
  - Proper verbal pacing and body movement
  - Properly manage allotted time
  - Reserve time for rebuttal, if desired
  - Be totally familiar with client's and opponent's case
  - Be familiar with all authorities cited by either side
  - Avoid using notes
  - Attorney for plaintiff goes first
  - Ask judges if they need a recitation of the facts
  - Recite facts if necessary
  - Present argument in a coherent manner (attorney is to educate judge on the law)
  - Concede losing arguments when appropriate
  - Be prepared to answer questions from judges
  - Be honest with judges if you don't know an answer
  - Ask for appropriate relief

Section 6. Trial (Court / Jury)/Arbitration

A. Trial (Court / Jury)/Arbitration
  - By mutual agreement, preexisting contract, statute, or court order
  - Analyze case
    - Client's strengths and weaknesses
    - Opponent's strengths and weaknesses
  - Plan appropriate strategy
    - Become familiar with rules of arbitration
    - Informal or strict trial-like setting
    - Relaxed or strict evidentiary standards
    - Witness preparation
    - Opening statements and closing arguments
    - Witness examinations
    - Exhibits
  - Select neutral time and location for arbitration
    - Court appointed or selected by parties' agreement
    - Experience
    - Bias
    - Acceptable time and location for all concerned
    - Appropriate scheduling and total time allocation
    - Division/payment of arbitration/trial fees and facility costs

- Witness preparation
  - Explain arbitration/trial procedure
  - Instruct witness to tell the truth (answer "yes" or "no," do not volunteer information)
  - Outline of direct and expected cross-examinations
  - Demeanor and appearance
    - Clothing
    - Body language
    - Pace
    - Tone
    - Voice
  - Time and place of proceeding
  - Subpoena uncooperative witnesses, if allowed
  - Trial/arbitration notebooks should contain:
    - All pleadings, motions, discovery requests, and responses
    - Applicable substantive and procedural law
    - Trial briefs
    - Evidentiary objections
    - Witness statements or prior testimony
    - Voir dire questions
    - Outlines of direct and cross-examinations
    - Outlines of opening and closing statements
    - Jury instructions (when applicable)
- Statement of the case similar to trial brief, by attorneys
  - Advocacy document designed to persuade fact finder of case
  - Statement of the issues
  - Statement of facts
  - Applicable law
  - Theory of the case
  - Conclusion (relief requested)
  - Exhibit list (may be separate documents)
  - Witness list (may be separate documents)
- Joint statement of the case
  - Often required by judge/arbitrator
  - Establishes and narrows issues and areas of agreement and conflict
  - Focuses the presentation
  - May help with settlement
  - Assists judge/arbitrator in deciding case
- Exhibits
  - Marked as per judge's/arbitrator's procedure
  - Proper foundation
  - Accepted by judge/arbitrator
- Stipulations
  - Negotiated between parties and accepted by judge/arbitrator
  - Avoids argument over uncontested issues or facts
  - Jury selection (where applicable)
- Jury Selection (procedure varies—check local court rules.)
  - Introduction (attorneys, parties, witnesses)
  - Question jurors individually and as a panel

- o Have a workable system for charting response (e.g., clerk labels response by juror number)
- o Explain trial procedures
- o Gather relevant information about jurors
- o Educate jurors about client and theory of the case
- o Detect favorable and unfavorable bias
- o Challenges for cause
- o Pass the panel for cause
- o Peremptory challenges
- Opening statements
  - o Plaintiff/party with burden of proof goes first
  - o Appropriate appearance and demeanor
    - – Clothing
    - – Body language
    - – Pace
    - – Tone
    - – Voice
  - o Use appropriate visual aids
  - o Tell client s story
  - o Explain what will be proved
  - o Do not make promises that cannot be kept
  - o Ask for relief that client wants
  - o Avoid being argumentative
  - o Use proper verbal pacing, body motion, and eye contact
- Case-in-chief
  - o Plaintiff/party with burden of proof proceeds with its evidence first
    - – Call witnesses in strategic order
    - – Primacy and recency effects
    - – Logical order that will not be confusing
    - – Designed to provide maximum impact
  - o Direct examination
    - – Use appropriate demeanor
    - – Use effective structure
    - – Calm the nervous witness, if necessary
    - – Establish appropriate background information
    - – Establish credibility of witness
    - – Use appropriate leading questions (*See* F.R.E. 611(c))
    - – Avoid leading questions regarding important testimony
    - – Keep the scope of the examination focused
    - – Elicit all desired information from witness
    - – Use witness to identify and lay foundation for exhibits
    - – Have witness explain any harmful information
  - o Cross-examination
    - – Use appropriate demeanor
    - – Use effective structure
    - – Ask only leading questions
    - – Short questions
    - – Insist on one-word answers
    - – Be persistent

- Avoid arguing with the witness
- Do not ask a question if the answer is not known
- Impeach the credibility of the witness
- Undermine the witness's perception of events
- Point out inconsistencies with prior statements
- Point out inconsistencies with other witnesses testimony
- Emphasize information helpful to client

o Re-direct examination
- Limited to scope of cross-examination
- Rehabilitate the credibility of the witness
- Reestablish the witness perception of events
- Explain any inconsistencies
- Clarify any ambiguities or misstatements
- Use sparingly, do not repeat what has been covered
- Making appropriate objections
- Listen carefully to opponent's examination
- Consider the tactical or strategic implications of objecting
- Object promptly and decisively
- Follow correct procedure
- Briefly state a valid evidentiary reason for the objection
- Be prepared to counter opposing arguments

- Expert Witnesses
o Scope of expert examination
- Technical or other specialized knowledge of the expert will assist the fact finder in understanding evidence or in determining a fact that is in issue
o Who is the expert?
- A person with specialized knowledge by education, training, experience, or skill may be qualified as an expert; professionals who have extensive formal education and training may be readily qualified, such as doctors, engineers, and economists.
o Areas of expertise
- An area of knowledge that contains scientific, technical, or other specialized information may constitute an admissible area of expertise
o The law of expert testimony
- Federal Rule of Evidence 702
- Federal Rule of Evidence 705
- *Daubert v. Merrell Dow Pharmaceuticals*, 509 U.S. 579 (1993)
- *Frye v. United States*, 293 F.1013 (D.C. Cir. 1923)
o Qualifying the expert
- Expert has education, training, experience, or skill beyond general knowledge of the fact finder
- Expert has sufficient information on which to testify in the particular case
- Expert opinion is based on education, training, experience, and skill of the expert as applied to the information and not on unfounded speculation or conjecture

- Direct Examination (see also direct examination generally)
o Purpose
- Provide fact finder with factual information
- Apply expert knowledge to the facts and render an opinion
- Explain scientific principles and theories

- Explain test procedures and results
- Explain real evidence introduced in the case
- Interpret facts and render an opinion regarding the likelihood of an event
- Explain the amount of recoverable damages in a civil case
- Give an opinion that contradicts the conclusions of an expert for the opposing party
  - Outline of expert direct examination
    - Subject matter of the opinion
    - Theories or principles that support the area of expertise and opinion
    - Sources of information relied upon by the expert
    - Standard tests or procedures used in a case
    - Other basis of the opinion of the expert
    - The opinion of conclusion
    - Explanation of the opinion and conclusion
    - Identify sources of information
    - Personal, firsthand information perceived prior to the trial or hearing
    - Information obtained from experts, documents, records, files, witnesses, and other sources prior to or during the trial or hearing
    - Evidence including testimony heard by or told to the expert during the case
    - Hypothetical questions
- Cross-Examination (*see also* cross-examination generally)
  - Preparing and presenting an effective supporting and discrediting cross-examination of an expert witness that includes:
    - Categories/Factors of Expert Cross-Examination
    - Supportive Cross-Examination
- Obtain concessions
  - Criticize the other side's positions
    - Discrediting cross-examination
      - Disclose expert fees and financial interests
      - Establish bias or prejudice
      - Attack sources of information
      - Show unreliable or insufficient information
      - Dispute facts
      - Show lack of thoroughness
      - Show insufficient testing
      - Attack validity and reliability of test
      - Establish existence of other causes
      - Show inappropriate or insufficient expertise
      - Establish differences of opinion among experts
      - Establish subjective opinions
      - Introduce inconsistent prior statements
      - Discredit hypothetical questions
      - Expose other deficiencies
      - Expose unreliability of expertise
      - Use conflicting treatises
  - Responding to objections
    - Stop the testimony
    - Listen carefully to opponent's objection
    - Offer an appropriate response

Darngood v. Landers and PUDS, Plaintiff

- Continue if objection is overruled
- Try another approach if objection is sustained
- o Closing Arguments
  - Plaintiff/party with burden of proof goes last (in some jurisdictions, plaintiff argues first, then defendant, followed by plaintiff's rebuttal)
  - Use proper verbal pacing, body motion/language, eye contact, tone, and voice
  - Be persuasive and compelling
  - Use appropriate visual aids
  - Explain why the law supports the client's case
  - Tell why the client should win
  - Tell why the opposing client should lose
  - Explain how the verdict form should be completed
- o Jury instructions (where appropriate)
  - Before or after closing arguments, or combination (in complex and long trials, instructions may be read during the trial)
  - Listen carefully as judge instructs jury
  - Ask to approach bench if judge misinstructs jury

LEARNING OBJECTIVES

The Learning Objectives provide a method to measure achievement.

- **Oral**—the oral learning objectives assist in planning and delivering the assigned oral skill.

- **Written**—the written learning objectives assist in the development and presentation of both written and oral skills.

TRIAL (Court/Jury)—ARBITRATION
ORAL

Oral Objective A—Trial/Arbitration
- Demonstrate effective advocacy skills in a trial/arbitration, including effective procedure and practice.
- Oral Objective A is achieved by:
  - preparing, practicing, and presenting opening statements, direct examinations, cross-examinations, and final argument
  - preparing witnesses and exhibits
  - representing the client at a prehearing conference
  - representing a client—opening statement and closing argument, direct examination, and cross-examination of witnesses
  - developing a trial/arbitration notebook

Oral Objective B—Opening Statement
- Demonstrate an understanding of effective opening statement strategy and skills.
- Oral Objective B is achieved by:
  - preparing and presenting an opening statement that demonstrates:
    - effective organization and structure
    - effective storytelling
    - a clear explanation of the theory of the case
    - effective use of persuasive approaches and techniques
    - effective explanation of weaknesses in case
    - effective delivery and presentation
    - avoidance of objectionable and argumentative opening statement
  - demonstrating an understanding of personal strengths and weaknesses by clearly articulating:
    - areas where attorney wants feedback
    - techniques that will be used
    - risks and experiments to be taken
    - personal strengths and weaknesses

Oral Objective C—Direct Examination
- Demonstrate an understanding of effective direct examination strategy and skills.
- Oral Objective C is achieved by:
  - preparing and presenting a direct examination that demonstrates:
    - a detailed story (for the portion of the examination conducted)
    - questions that solicit sufficient foundation and detail

- an ability to deliver an interesting and persuasive story
- simple, understandable questions
- nonobjectionable questions and responses
- understanding evidentiary rules and purpose of objections
- effective structure—examination conducted in a chronological or orderly fashion
- effective pace and follow-up—listening and clarifying answers
- appropriate demeanor and presence—eye contact, voice projection, facial expressions, gestures, physical posture, and avoidance of distractions
    o clearly articulating:
- areas where attorney wants feedback
- techniques that will be used
- risks and experiments to be taken
- personal strengths and weaknesses

Oral Objective D—Cross-Examination
- Demonstrate an understanding of effective cross-examination strategy and skills.
- Oral Objective D is achieved by:
    o preparing and presenting a cross-examination that demonstrates:
        - effective leading questions
        - sufficient and appropriate details
        - questions and delivery that hold the interest of the fact finder
        - simple questions that are understandable
        - questions that are appropriate—not argumentative, not objectionable
        - understanding evidentiary rules, evidentiary objections, and understanding of objections
        - effective structure—thematic, chronological, orderly
        - effective follow-up, listening, and clarifying answers
        - demeanor and presence—appropriate eye contact, voice projection, facial expressions, gestures, physical posture, and avoidance of distractions
    o demonstrating an understanding of personal strengths and weaknesses by clearly articulating:
        - areas where attorney wants feedback
        - techniques that will be used
        - risks and experiments to be taken
        - personal strengths and weaknesses

Oral Objective E—Closing Argument
- Demonstrate an understanding of effective closing argument strategy and skills.
- Oral Objective E is achieved by:
    o preparing and presenting a closing argument that demonstrates:
        - persuasiveness—effective presentation
        - interest—developed and maintained interest
        - organization—presentation well organized
        - balance—appropriate balance of facts, law, reasons
        - demeanor and presence—appropriate eye contact, voice projection, facial expressions, gestures, physical posture, and avoidance of distractions
        - avoidance of objectionable summation

    o demonstrating an understanding of personal strengths and weaknesses by clearly articulating:
- areas where attorney wants feedback
- techniques that will be used
- risks and experiments to be taken
- personal strengths and weaknesses

WRITTEN

Written Objective A—Trial (Court/Jury) —Arbitration
- Identify and analyze the legal issues involved in representing a client including:
  - the basic law involved in the exercise
  - the essential facts, the client's position, applicable law, initial research and supporting arguments, and the relevant rules and procedures involved in this exercise
- Provide a framework for analyzing the client's case, which includes:
  - a preliminary opinion as to the likelihood of success
- Written Objective A is achieved by:
  - [*Six-page limit*]
  - writing a case analysis based on the procedural and substantive law governing the law provided in this exercise that demonstrates:
    - a clear and complete understanding of each party's theory of the case
    - a clear and complete understanding of themes for each party
    - an understanding of the elements necessary for each party to prevail at the trial/arbitration
    - an understanding of the weaknesses and strengths of each party's case
    - an understanding of appropriate remedies

Written Objective B—Opening Statement
- Demonstrate an understanding of effective opening statement strategy and skills.
- Written Objective B is achieved by:
  - [*Three-page limit*]
  - preparing a written analysis of the opening statement that demonstrates an understanding of the following:
    - the specific approach to the opening statement
    - how the opening fits the theory of the case
    - how the opening is consistent with the closing
    - the structure of the opening
  - [*One-page limit*]
  - demonstrating an understanding of personal strengths and weaknesses by clearly articulating:
    - areas where attorney wants feedback
    - techniques that will be used
    - risks and experiments to be taken
    - personal strengths and weaknesses

Written Objective C—Direct Examination
- Demonstrate an understanding of effective direct examination strategy and skills.
- Written Objective C is achieved by:

  [*Three-page limit*]
  - preparing a written analysis of the assigned direct examination that demonstrates the following:
    - the specific approach to this direct examination
    - how the direct examination fits the theory of the case
    - addressing the strengths and weaknesses of the witness
    - an effective structure of the direct examination

  [*One-page limit*]
  - demonstrating an understanding of personal strengths and weaknesses by clearly articulating:
    - areas where attorney wants feedback
    - techniques that will be used
    - risks and experiments to be taken
    - personal strengths and weaknesses

Written Objective D—Cross-Examination
- Demonstrate an understanding of effective cross-examination strategy and skills.
- Written Objective D is achieved by:

  [*Three-page limit*]
  - preparing a written analysis of the assigned cross-examination that demonstrates the following:
    - the specific approach to this cross-examination
    - how the cross-examination fits the theory of the case
    - addressing the strengths and weaknesses of the witness
    - an effective structure of the cross-examination

  [*One-page limit*]
  - demonstrating an understanding of personal strengths and weaknesses by clearly articulating:
    - areas where attorney wants feedback
    - techniques that will be used
    - risks and experiments to be taken
    - personal strengths and weaknesses

Written Objective E—Closing Argument
- Demonstrate an understanding of effective closing argument strategy and skills.
- Written Objective E is achieved by:

  [*Three-page limit*]
  - preparing a written analysis of the assigned closing argument that demonstrates
    - the specific approach to the closing
    - how the closing fits the theory of the case
    - how the closing is consistent with the opening
    - an effective structure
    - how the evidence will be explained to the fact finder
    - the techniques to tell an interesting and compelling story

    – how to explain to the fact finder what the case is all about including theories, issues, claims, defenses, and positions

    – how to persuade the fact finders of the merits of the case

    – how to motivate the fact finder to want to render a favorable verdict

[*One-page limit*]

  o demonstrating an understanding of personal strengths and weaknesses by clearly articulating:

    – areas where attorney wants feedback

    – techniques that will be used

    – risks and experiments to be taken

    – personal strengths and weaknesses

DEPOSITIONS

ORAL

Oral Objective A—Taking a Deposition

- Demonstrate effective deposition skills, including:
  - the ability to ask appropriate and sufficiently detailed questions with appropriate follow-up to obtain necessary information
  - the ability to control witness and guide the pace and scope of the deposition
- Oral Objective A is achieved by
  - implementing a deposition plan
  - assessing the relevant issues of the case
  - evaluating the witness's ability to provide valuable information
  - engaging in fact finding by asking appropriate questions—either open or closed ended
  - eliciting all necessary information—good or bad—from each deponent

Oral Objection B—Defending a Deposition

- Demonstrate effective client defense skills, including:
  - the ability to support and protect the witness during deposition
  - the ability to preserve and clarify the testimony produced during deposition
- Oral Objective B is achieved by:
  - providing emotional support for client through appropriate preparation and counseling
  - preserving the record through appropriate objections
  - protecting client's interests through clarification of testimony during cross-exam
  - ensuring adequate counseling through conferral during depositions

Oral Objective C—Individual Analysis

- Demonstrate an understanding of personal strengths and weaknesses
- Oral Objective C is achieved by clearly articulating:
  - areas where attorney wants feedback
  - techniques and strategies that will be used
  - risks and experiments to be taken
  - personal strengths and weaknesses

DEPOSITIONS

WRITTEN

Written Objective A—Identifying and Analyzing Issues

- Identify and analyze the legal and equitable issues inherent in this dispute between potential litigants, specifically demonstrating:
  o an understanding of a framework for evaluating the dispute
  o an understanding of legal principles
  o an understanding of state statutory law, local government ordinances and regulations, case law, and public policy concerns
  o the ability to identify and formulate a plan for resolving issues in a negotiation involving non-monetary interests
  o the ability to identify and formulate applicable legal issues and theories
  o the ability to identify the appropriate questions necessary to elicit information pertinent to the theory of the case
  o the techniques that will be used to achieve the goals for the deposition
- Written Objection A is achieved by:
  [*Four-page limit*]
  o writing a memorandum to a senior partner providing an analysis based on the fact and research of procedures, statutes, regulations, and case law, in the participant's jurisdiction that demonstrates:
    – the specific approach to the deposition
    – a clear and complete understanding of each party's theory of the case
    – a clear and complete understanding of the themes for each party
    – an understanding of the elements necessary for each party to prevail at the trial
    – an understanding of the weakness and strength of each party's case
    – an understanding of appropriate remedies
  o preparing a memorandum to a senior partner describing the results of the deposition and how the results were consistent with/inconsistent with and were affected by the deposition plan and the other party

NEGOTIATION

ORAL

Oral Objective A—Negotiation

- Demonstrate effective strategy and negotiation skills.
- Oral Objective A is achieved by:
  o Resolving conflicts by negotiating with opposing counsel/interested third parties
  o Implementing client goals in accord with interests
  o Conveying client needs/interests to opposing counsel
  o Applying style, strategies, and negotiation plan
  o Generating maximum creative problem-solving options
  o Evaluating with opposing counsel their gains/losses from alternate options
  o Ignoring, exposing, ruling out, or responding to inappropriate negotiation tactics
  o Narrowing opposing counsel's focus to the win-win option(s)
  o Perfecting and obtaining agreement on settlement details

Oral Objective B—Individual Analysis
- Demonstrate an understanding of personal strengths and weaknesses.
- Oral Objective B is achieved by clearly articulating:
  - SWOR analysis (strengths, weaknesses, opportunities, risks)
  - Opportunities passed or taken
  - End results of risks and experiments
  - Techniques that will be used
  - Areas where attorney wants feedback

WRITTEN

Written Objective A—Identifying and Analyzing Issues
- Specify and analyze the legal and equitable issues involved in representing a client.
- Written Objective A is achieved by:
  [Four-page limit]
  - Writing a memorandum to a senior partner providing an analysis based on research of procedural and substantive law that demonstrates a clear, complete understanding of:
    - the elements necessary to reach an agreement in client's best interests
    - the theory and themes of the case
    - the strengths, weaknesses, opportunities, and risks of the case
    - appropriate remedies
    - expertise in pertinent basic case and statutory law, ordinances, regulations, and public policy
    - an effective pre-negotiation outline
    - knowledge of relevant facts, client's position, supporting research/arguments, and applicable rules/procedures
    - a plan for a negotiation allowing for relevant third-party interests
    - a framework for case analysis, including:
      - theory of likelihood of success
      - cooperative or adversarial problem resolution
      - legal and nonlegal theories and arguments
      - plan allowing for third-party interest
  [Four-page limit]
  - Writing a memorandum to a senior partner detailing the negotiation results and evaluating their consistency and effects from the negotiation plan.

Written Objective B—Negotiation Planning
- Demonstrate effective negotiation strategies and techniques in the negotiation plan.
- Written Objective B is achieved by:
  [Three-page limit]
  - Preparation of a negotiation plan that:
    - clarifies all elements of the plan
    - is legally astute and uses good judgment
    - is structurally sound/organized
    - uses clear/concise plain language

Darngood v. Landers and PUDS, Plaintiff

- employs impact words and phrases
- addresses strengths, weaknesses, opportunities, and risks
- anticipates problems including third-party interests
- considers legal/procedural ramifications
- applies law to relevant facts
- supports a maximum fair settlement in accord with client needs
- allows for relief requested
- encompasses confidentiality provisions
- facilitates future relations, if that is a goal

MEDIATION

ORAL

Oral Objective A—Mediation

- Demonstrate effective mediation strategy and skills.
- Oral Objective A is achieved by:
  o Conferencing between counsel or with mediator pre-mediation
  o Applying facilitative or evaluative style, strategies, plan
  o Deciding objective standards, i.e., custom, industry practice, or ethical norms
  o Ascertaining and conveying client needs/interests to opposing parties and counsel
  o Implementing party's goals in accord with interests
  o Helping parties realistically value the case
  o Generating maximum creative problem-solving options
  o Evaluating opposing party's/counsel's gains and losses from alternate options
    - "trashing" (tear apart weaknesses to give parties a reality check)
    - "bashing" (at initial offers with goal of settling somewhere in the middle)
    - "hashing it out" (encourage direct communication between parties)
    - free-form brainstorming with parties (suspending judgment)
    - conditional proposals
    - Socratic questioning to expose weak proposals/positions
    - questions to facilitate agreement
    - creating movement toward settlement
  o Caucusing, at mediator's discretion
  o Narrowing opposing counsel's focus to win-win option(s)
  o Obtaining/perfecting agreement on settlement including payment in kind, installment payments, abiding by third-party expertise, and apology
  o Obtaining buy-in of opposing counsel and interested third parties who could affect post-agreement compliance
  o Forging and finalizing terms of agreement

Oral Objective B—Individual Analysis

- Demonstrate an understanding of personal strengths and weaknesses.
- Oral Objective B is achieved by clearly articulating:
  o SWOR analysis (strengths, weaknesses, opportunities, risks)

- o Opportunities passed or taken
- o End results of risks and experiments
- o Techniques that will be used
- o Areas in which attorney wants feedback

WRITTEN

Written Objective A—Identifying and Analyzing Issues
- Specify and analyze the legal and equitable issues involved in representing a client.
- Written Objective A is achieved by:
  [*Four-page limit*]
  - o Writing a memorandum to a senior partner providing an analysis based on research of procedural and substantive law that demonstrates a clear, complete understanding of:
    - – the elements necessary to reach an agreement in client's best interests
    - – the theory and themes of the case
    - – the strengths, weaknesses, opportunities, and risks of the case
    - – appropriate remedies
    - – expertise in pertinent basic case and statutory law, ordinances, regulations, and public policy
    - – an effective pre-mediation outline
    - – knowledge of relevant facts, client's position, supporting research/arguments, and applicable rules/procedures
    - – a plan for a mediation allowing for relevant third-party interests
    - – a framework for case analysis, including:
      - ▪ theory of likelihood of success
      - ▪ cooperative or adversarial problem resolution
      - ▪ legal and nonlegal theories and arguments
  [*Four-page limit*]
  - o Writing a memorandum to a senior partner detailing the mediation results and evaluating their consistency and effects from the mediation plan.

Written Objective B—Mediation Planning
- Demonstrate effective mediation strategies and techniques in the mediation plan.
- Written Objective B is achieved by:
  [*Three-page limit*]
  - o Preparation of a mediation plan that:
    - – clarifies all elements of the plan
    - – is legally astute and uses good judgment
    - – is structurally sound/organized
    - – uses clear/concise plain language
    - – employs impact words and phrases
    - – addresses strengths, weaknesses, opportunities, and risks
    - – anticipates problems including third-party interests
    - – considers legal/procedural ramifications
    - – applies law to relevant facts
    - – supports a maximum fair settlement in accord with client needs

- allows for relief requested
- encompasses confidentiality provisions
- facilitates future relations, if that is a goal

MOTIONS / ORAL ARGUMENT
ORAL

Oral Objective A—Motion/Oral Argument
- Demonstrate effective motion/oral argument strategy and skills.
- Oral Objective A is achieved by:
  o preparing and presenting a motion/oral argument that demonstrates:
    - how the argument relates to the brief
    - how to deal with the strengths and weaknesses
    - how to deal with the opponent's argument
    - how to respond to questions
    - how to balance law and facts
    - persuasiveness—effective presentation
    - interest—developed and maintained interest
    - organization—presentation well organized
    - balance—appropriate balance of facts, law, reasons
    - responses to questions—appropriate answers
    - demeanor and presence—appropriate eye contact, voice projection, facial expressions, gestures, physical posture, and avoidance of distractions
    - avoidance of objectionable argument

Oral Objective B—Individual Analysis
- Demonstrate an understanding of personal strengths and weaknesses.
- Oral Objective B is achieved by clearly articulating:
    - areas where attorney wants feedback
    - techniques that will be used
    - risks and experiments to be taken
    - personal strengths and weaknesses

WRITTEN

Written Objective A—Identifying and Analyzing Issues
- Identify and analyze the legal issues involved in representing a client in a motion/oral argument, including:
  o the basic law involved in this exercise and
  o the essential facts, the client's position, applicable law, initial research and supporting arguments, and the relevant rules and procedures involved in this exercise.
- Provide a framework for analyzing the client's case, which includes:
  o a preliminary opinion as to the likelihood of success
- Written Objective A is achieved by:
    [*Four-page limit*]

o writing a memorandum to a senior partner providing an analysis based on the procedural and substantive law that demonstrates:
  − an understanding of the elements necessary to prevail at the hearing
  − a clear and complete understanding of the theory of the case
  − a clear and complete understanding of themes
  − an understanding of the weakness and strength of the case
  − an understanding of appropriate remedies

Written Objective B—Analysis of Argument and Brief/Memorandum

- Demonstrate an understanding of effective motion/oral argument and written argument strategy and skills.
- Written Objective B is achieved by:
  [Three-page limit]
  o preparing a written analysis of the motion/oral argument and brief that demonstrates an understanding of the following:
    − the specific approach to the brief and oral argument
    − how the argument fits the theory of the case
    − the structure of the oral argument
    − how to present a persuasive brief and oral argument
    − the techniques that will be used
- Demonstrate an understanding of effective appellate brief writing skills.
- Demonstrate an effective and persuasive use of facts, law, transcribed record, and other evidence.

Written Objective C—Brief/Memorandum

- Written Objective C is achieved by:
  [Ten-page limit]
  o preparing, filing, and serving a written appellate brief in the support of client's position that is:
    − clear
    − structured/organized
    − simply written in plain English
    − uses impact words
    − deals with strengths and weaknesses
    − applies law to facts
    − offers solutions/options
    − presents the relief requested

EXPERT WITNESSES

ORAL

Oral Objective A—Direction Examination

- Demonstrate an understanding of effective expert witness direct examination strategy and skills in a trial setting.
- Oral Objective A is achieved by:
  o Preparing and presenting a direct examination of an expert witness that demonstrates:
    − a detailed story (for the portion of the examination conducted)

- questions that solicit sufficient foundation and detail
- questions and delivery that hold the interest of the fact finder
- simple, understandable questions and responses
- understanding evidentiary rules, evidentiary objections, and purpose of objections
- effective structure—examination conducted in a chronological, thematic, orderly fashion
  o Preparing and presenting an effective direct examination of an expert witness that:
    - provides fact finder with factual information
    - applies expert knowledge to the facts and renders an opinion
    - explains scientific principles and theories
    - explains test procedures and results
    - explains real evidence introduced in the case
    - interprets facts and renders an opinion regarding the likelihood of an event
    - explains the amount of recoverable damages in a civil case
    - gives an opinion that contradicts the conclusions of an expert for the opposing party
  o Clearly articulating:
    - areas where attorney wants feedback
    - techniques that will be used
    - risks and experiments to be taken
    - personal strengths and weaknesses

Oral Objective B—Cross-Examination
- Demonstrate an understanding of effective expert witness cross-examination strategy and skills.
- Oral Objective B is achieved by:
  o Preparing and presenting a cross-examination that demonstrates:
    - effective leading questions
    - sufficient and appropriate details
    - questions and delivery that hold the interest of the fact finder
    - simple questions that are understandable
    - questions that are appropriate—not argumentative, not objectionable
    - understanding evidentiary rules, evidentiary objections, and purpose of objections
    - effective structure—thematic, chronological, orderly
    - effective follow-up, listening, and clarifying answers
    - demeanor and presence—appropriate eye contact, voice projection, facial expressions, gestures, physical posture, and avoidance of distractions
  o Preparing and presenting an effective supporting and discrediting cross-examination of an expert witness that:
    - utilizes categories/factors of expert cross-examination
      - supportive cross-examination
        * obtains information that supports the case, facts, witnesses, and themes
        * obtains concessions
        * criticizes the other side's positions
      - discrediting cross-examination
        * discloses expert fees and financial interests
        * establishes bias or prejudice
        * attacks sources of information
        * shows unreliable or insufficient information
        * disputes facts

    * shows lack of thoroughness
    * shows insufficient testing
    * establishes existence of other causes
    * shows inappropriate or insufficient expertise
    * establishes differences of opinion among experts
    * establishes subjective opinions
    * introduces inconsistent prior statements
    * discredits hypothetical questions
    * exposes other's deficiencies

- o Demonstrating an understanding of personal strengths and weaknesses by clearly articulating:
  - − areas where attorney wants feedback
  - − techniques that will be used
  - − risks and experiments to be taken
  - − personal strengths and weaknesses

WRITTEN

Written Objective A—Direct Examination

- Demonstrate an understanding of effective expert witness direct examination strategy and skills.
- Written Objectives A is achieved by:
  [Three-page limit]
  - o preparing a written analysis of the assigned direct examination that demonstrates the following:
    - − the specific approach to this direct examination
    - − how the direct examination fits the theory of the case
    - − dealing with strengths and weaknesses of the witness
    - − an effective structure of the direct examination

  [One-page limit]
  - o demonstrating an understanding of personal strengths and weaknesses by clearly articulating:
    - − areas where attorney wants feedback
    - − techniques that will be used
    - − risks and experiments to be taken
    - − personal strengths and weaknesses

Written Objective B—Expert Witness Cross-Examination

- Demonstrate an understanding of effective expert witness cross-examination strategy and skills.
- Written Objective B is achieved by:
  [Three-page limit]
  - o preparing a written analysis of the assigned cross-examination that demonstrates the following:
    - − the specific approach to this cross-examination
    - − how the cross-examination fits the theory of the case
    - − dealing with strengths and weaknesses of the witness
    - − an effective structure of the cross-examination

  [One -page limit]
  - o demonstrating an understanding of personal strengths and weaknesses by clearly articulating:
    - − areas where attorney wants feedback
    - − techniques that will be used

- risks and experiments to be taken
- personal strengths and weaknesses

Written Objective C—Individual Analysis
- Demonstrate an understanding of personal strengths and weaknesses.
- Written Objective C is achieved by clearly articulating:
    - areas where attorney wants feedback
    - techniques that will be used
    - risks and experiments to be taken
    - personal strengths and weaknesses